CHAPTER 1
FUNDAMENTALS OF DESIGN

1.1 GENERAL

Building a model railroad takes much time, work, and expense. The result is well worth it if the final effect is realistic and operation interesting. However excellent craftsmanship cannot overcome poor planning. Since the effort expended in examining the various possibilities and in preparing a well thought-out plan is small in comparison to that required for construction, design is a step which should be done with care.

This Chapter covers the broad factors which should be considered before any detailed planning is undertaken. Each fundamental is covered in depth in later chapters but it is important to avoid becoming inhibited by details in the early stages. In short, be sure you see the forest before looking at the trees.

Even the smallest layout can be built to represent a realistic part of some railroad and to be operated in a manner duplicating the prototype. This Handbook is devoted to the design of model *railroads*, not to designing tracks for running trains over a series of alternate routes. Little emphasis has been placed on designing for fixed-radius sectional track except in Chapter 8, the design of small layouts. Fixed-radius track sections can always be used but they introduce unnecessary restrictions if used exclusively.

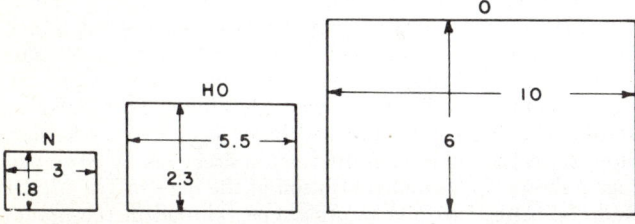

Fig. 1 Relative area for identical layouts

1.2 SPACE AVAILABLE VERSUS SCALE

The amount of railroad possible in a given area is inversely proportional to the square of the scale ratio. To duplicate a given N scale layout in HO would take 3.4 times as much area, in O, 11.1 times as much. The relative layout area required for these three scales is shown in Fig. 1. Access space, however, is based on people, not scale.

Space is a controlling factor with respect to scale only if the available space is so limited as to make an operating layout in a large scale impractical. For example an O scale layout in a space 1' by 6' (.3x1.8m) would be trivial, essentially serving only as a scenic setting for cars and locomotives. On the other hand a reasonable switching line could be built in N scale in that same area. In most cases, however, available space permits a layout in any of the popular scales provided the type of railroad and its extent are selected to suit. A 5' by 9' (1.5x2.7m) rectangle is about the smallest in which an HO layout representing a main line can be built, yet a O scale traction or narrow gauge line could also be built in that same area.

Often overlooked is that the reach of operators does not change with scale. As described in Section 3.2, easy access to all tracks from aisles or benchwork edges is vital. In some styles of benchwork this might limit radii to a maximum of 36" (91cm), excellent for N, reasonable for HO but limiting for O scale standard railroad equipment.

1.3 LIMITATION OF MANPOWER

The hours of maintenance required for large layouts are often underestimated. It is important that the capabilities of the available manpower for either operation or maintenance not be exceeded. Although size, particularly length of track and number of switches, is an important factor, curved turnouts, poor accessability, and other similar features under the control of the designer also affect the need for maintenance. The quality of workmanship and choice of materials for construction are very important. Dimensionally-unstable materials and poor practices can easily make a ten-fold increase in the hours of maintenance required; the same applies to wiring. This Handbook, however, is confined good design and the reduction of maintenance through avoiding known problem-producers. Information on sound trackwork construction can be found in the Trackwork Handbook for Model Railroads published by the Boynton & Associates, Clifton House, Clifton, VA. 22024 and on trouble-free wiring in the Electrical Handbook for Model Railroads by the same publisher as this Handbook. Both are by the author of this book.

Successful large layouts have been built by experienced model railroaders who have solved the manpower problem by operating almost as if the home layout was a club. It is recommended, however, that first home layouts be small, see Chapter 8. Nevertheless layouts should not be under-designed and one time-proven approach is to provide for expansion at a later date (Section 7.8).

1.4 THE BASIS FOR DESIGN

The touchstone of layout design is the concept of the railroad. A believable, realistic, and interesting model railroad can be built in any space providing it represents a consistent prototype scene suitable to that space. A carefully-developed concept of the prototype being modeled, that is its assumed era, location, type of traffic, etc., is the guide to realism (Chapter 2).

Design standards for reliable operation should be set early including such matters as minimum radii and maximum grades (Chapter 6). It cannot be overemphasized that the highest practical standards should be set. Reliable operation is worth more than squeezing in a few extra tracks.

Benchwork, its type of construction and height, places limitations on layout design. Select a benchwork design which best suits the proposed railroad. The benchwork is for the railroad, not the railroad for the benchwork. Do not allow a preconceived idea about benchwork prevent evaluating other types of benchwork against the requirements of the chosen track plan (Chapter 3).

Electrical control systems also place limitations on layout design (Chapter 5). However, unlike benchwork type, the control system intimately affects the operation of the layout. Some systems, walkaround cab control for example, place stringent requirements on layout planning.

Scenery is not a detail to be left until the tracks are planned. For realism and interest its requirements should be considered at all stages of planning including the very first (Chapter 4).

The facilities for prototype-like operation must be considered constantly. Way freights cannot be operated if there is no freight along the way (Chapters 10 through 14).

CHAPTER 2
CONCEPT OF RAILROAD

2.1 GENERAL

The concept of the railroad is the most important single design factor. Everything else depends heavily on it. Therefore the concept should be developed, at least in general terms, before even the most preliminary stages of planning.

Although there is great freedom in choosing a concept, that freedom is not unlimited. It would be absurd to imagine a heavy-traffic transcontinental railroad in a space 4' by 8' (1.2 x 2.4m) regardless of scale. The limiting factors of available space and manpower must be taken into account but within those limits there are many choices and none can be called 'best.' A space 6' by 10' (1.8 x 3m) could be used equally effectively in HO for a model of a logging line, an industrial switching district, or one station on a main line. The important thing is to select some interesting concept which can be carried out to a realistic, believable result.

Initially the concept can be in broad terms, perhaps simply an industrial switching line somewhere in Ohio. Later, as the design progresses, the concept is refined. It may be found, for example, that it is unreasonable to allocate the necessary space to heavy industries so these become excluded from the concept thereby changing the character of the industrial area.

2.2 PURPOSE OF LAYOUT

The first question to be settled is the purpose for which the layout will be built. Is it only for the enjoyment of its owner and an occasional visitor or will it be displayed to the public? Will it attempt to satisfy many interests such as narrow gauge, traction, branch-line operation as well as main line, or is it for a specialized interest?

Large layouts can fulfill many purposes but the smallest are best designed with but one purpose in mind. This is illustrated in Fig. 1 for two layouts of identical area. The one on the left is for the display of moving trains in mountain scenery, the one on the right for operation at a single station. Attempting to serve several purposes on a layout this small results in serving all poorly.

Even on large layouts, some purposes are in conflict. At clubs in particular the need to have loops for continuous running at public shows is at odds with the best design to simulate a real railroad (Section 7.11).

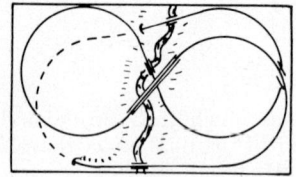 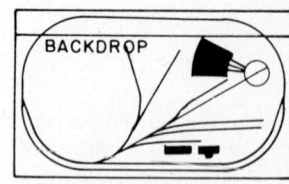

DISPLAY OF MOVING TRAINS   STATION OPERATION

Fig. 1 Purpose of layout

2.3 ASSUMED LOCATION OF RAILROAD

To be effective a model railroad must be believable. It should be a model *railroad*, not a miscellaneous collection of buildings, track, and scenery which makes no prototype sense. A crutch which is leaned on far too often is, 'There is a prototype for everything.' Real railroads are characterized by the usual, the odd being just that, something seldom seen. Model railroads are forced into enough strange conditions simply because the available space has corners and there never is enough room for prototype-like spacings and distances. The addition of unnecessary unusual features takes away from realism.

An excellent guide to an overall effect of realism is to assume a prototype location for the railroad and then attempt to conform to the actual scenes and practices of that area. Best results are obtained if the location assumed is one with which the modeler is familiar or is willing to gain a detailed knowledge. Railroads in the eastern US have a distinctly different flavor than those in the west; it is not just a matter of the size of mountains. Clubs, in particular, are well advised to base their layouts on the local region as the membership will change with the years. It is safer to assume that new members will have local knowledge and interests rather than of some remote area. As an example, Fig. 2 shows the assumed location of the lines of The Model Railroad Club, Inc. Every prototype railroad in the immediate vicinity of the club building has been included. The narrow gauge line indicated is of eastern prototype, specifically the East Broad Top, to be consistent with the rest of the railroad.

Just as most knowledgeable model railroaders are more impressed by a scratch-built model which is an exact duplicate of a PRR K4 than they are of a freelance 4-6-2, so visitors will find a model of a local station or some prominent building more interesting than just any building. Even if space does not permit a full-blown model, the flavor of the prototype often can be retained so that particular station or other structure is immediately recognizable.

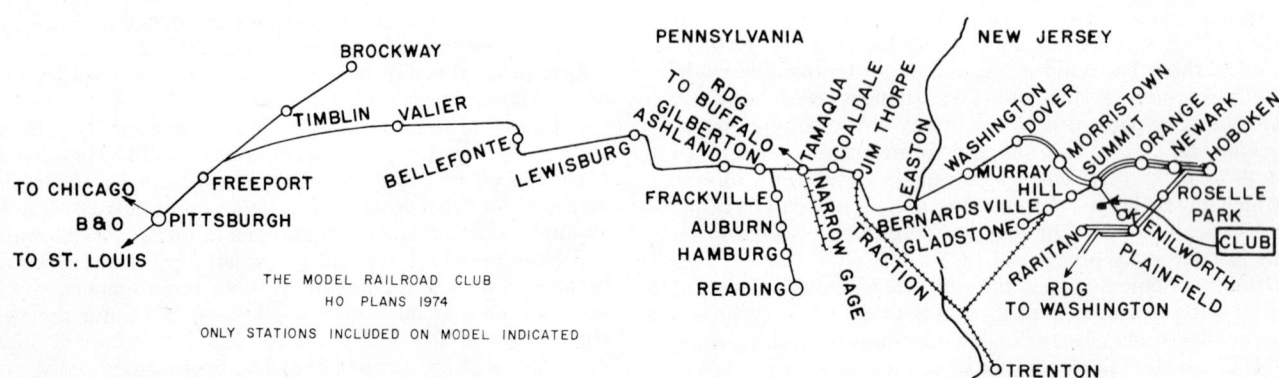

Fig. 2 Presumed prototype location of a model railroad

2.4 ERA AND SEASON

For maximum realism the era and season of any given model railroad scene should be consistent. It is easiest to build to the modern era for that is the best known. Probably clubs should adhere to the modern era, for, as the years pass, it may be difficult to recruit members interested in a particular period even though the founding group could agree on one.

An individual can select a particular date for his railroad. He then must be careful to avoid anything introduced after that date and this may be difficult as there are many subtle gradual changes, for example, when did cables start to replace open-wire telephone lines? Fortunately the reverse is not true, interesting old features can be included on a layout set in modern times. The B&O still operated in 1970 over a bridge built in 1826. However, to be believable, the old features must appear as though they had come down to modern times. It is conceivable that a narrow gauge line bringing coal to an interchange with a modern standard gauge railroad could still be economically viable but that narrow gauge line should appear to be in the same time setting as the main line, i.e., horses and buggies should not be pulled up in front of the narrow gauge stations with modern automobiles at the standard gauge stations.

On a layout which can be divided into scenically isolated units, the era could be changed from unit to unit but the time span could not be great as the trains would remain the same. This technique could be effectively used to include more than one season on a model railroad. Typically model railroads have a summer appearance however.

Lightweight rails on a well scenicked industrial spur on the HO layout of the New York Society of Model Engineers impart an old, rickety look. Track is actually very carefully laid and handles switching locomotives and cars smoothly and without derailments.

2.5 TYPE OF RAILROAD

Nothing is more important to the concept than the type of railroad to be modeled. The selection of type should be based on the form of operation and the class of equipment of greatest interest to the owner consistent with the size of layout contemplated. In this Handbook a large layout is defined as one in which several types of railroads can be realistically included such as the multiple and single-track main lines, heavy and light branch lines, traction, and narrow gauge. A medium-size layout typically must be confined to one major type of railroad but is large enough that even major realignments of tracks at one point on the layout do not require general modification of the entire layout. A small layout is defined as one in which the limitations of available space are controlling to the extent that the entire layout must be designed as a unit (Chapter 8). In any reasonable area just about any type of railroad can be successfully modeled provided a judicious selection of features is made.

Heavy Main Line

When the interest is in running long trains, some portion of a main line is a good choice. Even in a limited area a reasonable main line can be represented, providing only one facet is selected, e.g., a scenic part of a line, a single small station, or a small interlocking plant. One concept for main-line operation is a bridge line such as the Richmond, Fredericksburg & Potomac or the Atlanta & West Point, both shown in Fig. 3. Complete trains were turned over to such bridge lines, passenger as well as freight. Thus small interchange yards rather than large terminals are all that are required.

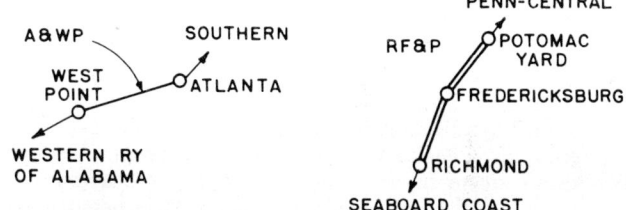

Fig. 3 Prototype bridge lines

Terminal Railroad

Another concept permitting the operation of major mainline trains is the terminal railroad. Such a line can serve as an intermediate switching line connecting line-haul carriers and thus justify locomotives and cabooses from several railroads on the same tracks. It could also (or only) operate the union passenger terminal. It might serve industries along its own tracks. Fig. 4 shows a portion of the Terminal Railroad Association of St. Louis, a very large prototype example of a terminal line. The number and variety of passenger trains out of its Union Station was once enormous. In 1971 it had direct connections with 16 trunk lines plus three switching lines, and had 101 locomotives to serve over 400 industries along its 341 miles of right of way.

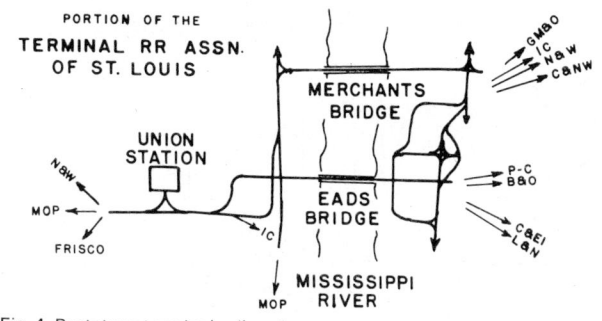

Fig. 4 Prototype terminal railroad

Belt Line

A belt line is a form of a terminal railroad which provides a line around the congested terminal area to speed interchange service between the line-haul carriers. The Indiana Harbor Belt Railroad shown in Fig. 5 is an example. Since belt lines not part of a terminal railroad typically do not include the major passenger terminal of the area, they rarely, perhaps never, handled major regularly-scheduled passenger trains of the line-haul carriers. However some did provide local passenger service. In 1905 the Indiana Harbor Belt operated 12 passenger trains daily. Some prototype railroads which are named belt lines, the San Francisco Belt RR was one, are not belt lines as defined here.

Short Line

Although applicable to a variety of railroads, the term short line generally is construed to mean a small railroad operated in a comparatively informal manner. Typically a short line originates and terminates traffic from and to its connections as does a switching line but usually has identifiable main tracks extending distances, often miles, between shippers. The Rahway Valley RR shown in Fig. 7 is an example of a short line in this sense.

Many short lines, including the Rahway Valley, once ran scheduled passenger trains, often as through trains with one of their connections. Even in 1976 some of the short lines operated steam passenger trains as tourist attractions, an example being the Morristown & Erie.

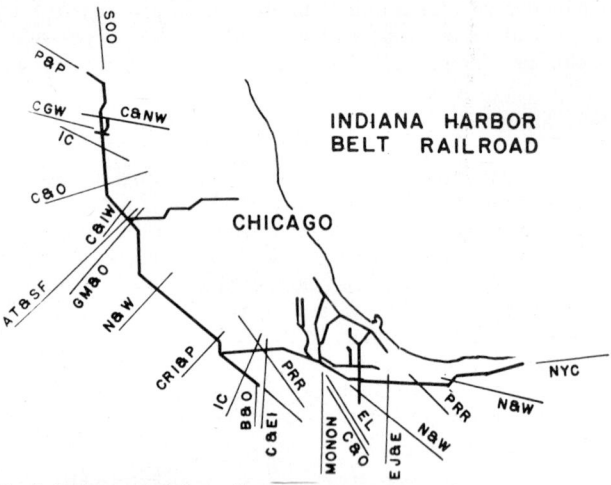

Fig. 5 Prototype belt-line railroad

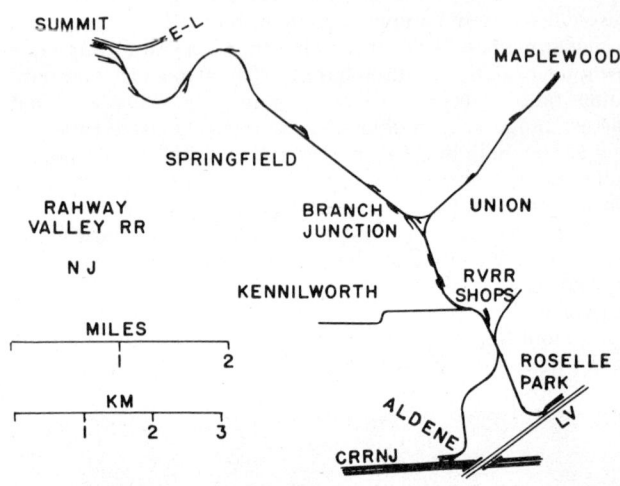

Fig. 7 Prototype short line

Switching Line

A switching line is a form of terminal railroad which primarily, often exclusively, originates and terminates traffic. As a concept it can provide the maximum amount of switching operations in any given space. It is particularly adapted to shelf railroads as there is no need for loops or ovals. Although trains are not operated, all forms of freight cars and their facilities can be justified including piggyback (TOFC). Fig. 6 shows a prototype switching line, the Hoboken Shore in N.J. as it existed in 1956. It even provided a limited amount of intermediate switching via its transfer bridge to car floats. This railroad was once electrified.

Special Railroads

The types of railroads described so far handle standard interchange freight cars. There are many types of railroads operated wholly or in part using special equipment. Interurban, street-car, and rapid transit lines are examples as well as railroads serving special industries such as logging or mining. Such railroads generally use tight radii and short cars and thus are excellent prototypes when space is limited. Often they are added as adjuncts to a model of a conventional railroad (Chapter 14).

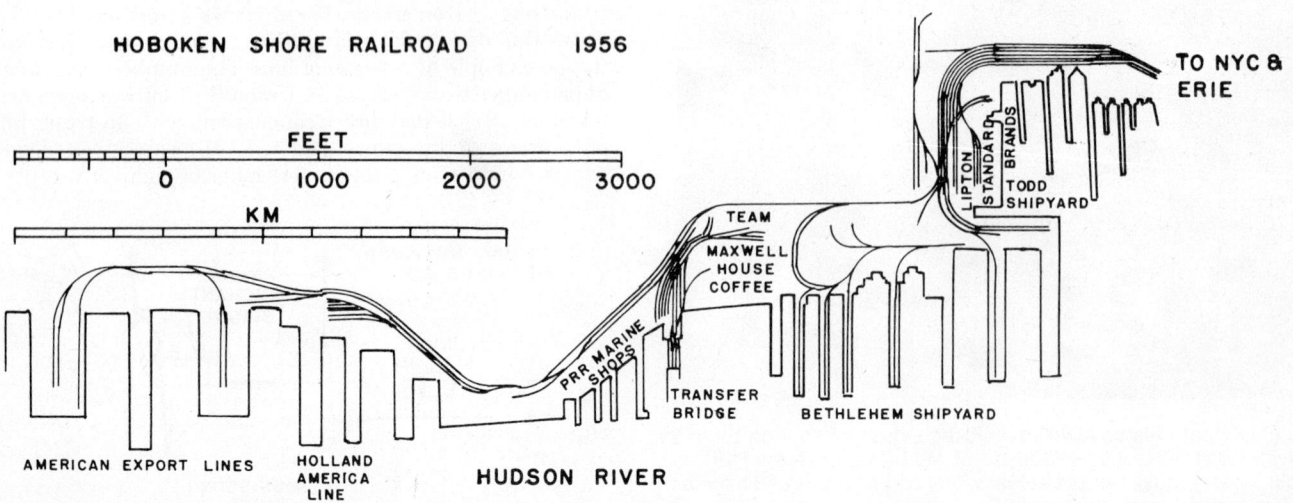

Fig. 6 Prototype switching railroad

2.6 CHOICE OF CONCEPT

To choose a concept all the factors described in this Chapter should be considered and weighed against each other. In particular the ability of the proposed layout to hold interest over the years should not be overlooked. Often, particularly on a first layout, too much emphasis is laid on the continuous running of trains or perhaps on having alternate routes available. Continuous running is a legitimate objective for layouts which are designed to be shown to the public or to be operated by children but just running trains in endless circles can become quite boring. Experience has shown that operation in the prototype manner is the key to continuity of interest. Therefore, when making the choice of concept, always view each possibility in the light of how it actually represents a real railroad and how it would be operated if it was indeed a real railroad.

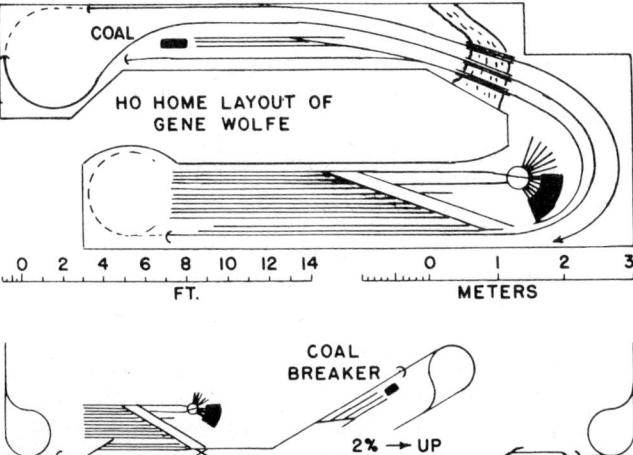

Fig. 8 Concept for a medium-size layout

A particularly well-developed concept for a home layout by Gene Wolfe is illustrated in Fig. 8. The setting is a narrow valley in the coal-mining area of Pennsylvania. The railroad is a portion of the main line with a small yard at the junction of a branch line and part of that branch line. Hidden wyes (reverse movement required) exist at the ends of the main and branch lines.

This concept permits a spectacular display of relatively long trains with helpers storming the grade to climb up and out of the valley as well as trains drifting down that lengthy grade. The sizable yard offers many possibilities of switching, one obvious example being the local interchange between mainline and branch trains. Way freights can order their cars for the next part of their run. Blocks of cars can be set out for a later train, e.g. by a through freight for a local or for a train presumed for a different route.

Although the space available was large as home layouts go, Gene Wolfe modeled a few features well, the coal breaker on the branch line is of scale size for instance, rather than crowding in many small features. To gain space the small station and helper facilities at the top of the grade as well as the reversing wye there are located on a second benchwork level (Fig. 12, Chapter 3).

Generating a concept for a small railroad generally means considering possible concepts which are suitable for the space available and also which fit the interests of the builder and then selecting one. On the other hand the concept for a large railroad is built step by step. In the case of the railroad shown in Fig. 2, the first decision made was to build a complete railroad with a long, mostly single-track main line from a large waterfront terminal to some western connection. Next it was decided to follow prototype tracks although not those of a single railroad. The prototype lines selected were those closest to the location of the model. This fixed the eastern terminal as Hoboken. After considering various possible western terminals such as Buffalo and Roanoke, Pittsburgh was selected as it seemed to offer the most logical reason for running major passenger trains. Even the large space available, 44' by 150' (13.4m by 45.7m), did not permit a western terminal large enough to accept the amount of traffic which could be generated by a near-scale Hoboken (Fig. 11, Chapter 10 and Fig. 12, Chapter 11) if the western terminal had to handle the inbound trains on a car-by-car basis. Therefore the concept called for an interchange yard at Pittsburgh (Fig. 7, Chapter 7) long enough to handle 80 to 90 car trains. Such trains would be turned over to the B&O, the presumption being the B&O would do the necessary switching in their yards. The concept at this point is shown in Fig. 9.

Fig. 9 Main-line concept

Since an almost-scale Hoboken, a major commuter terminal, was included, realism required that the concept include commuter lines. For variety, as shown in Fig. 2, both multi-track and single track commuter lines were planned, some electrified, others not. The small terminal at Raritan could not justify significant freight service down the multi-track branch (on the prototype the CRRNJ main line). Consequently the concept included a scale model of the interchange with the Reading at Bound Brook Junction. Pool freights to and from the south use this junction on the prototype and therefore can be realistically included on the model. As indicated in Fig. 10, these trains have as their other terminal a small interchange yard at Tamaqua where they conceptually are trains from Buffalo. Thus they provide additional traffic on the main line.

As a concept develops, it is refined to make it more consistent with the assumed prototype and to add interesting features, both operational and scenic. In the case illustrated above a long 2½% grade was introduced not only to justify helper service but also to require it for long trains. On a small or medium size layout probably only one facility can be included of a type, for example TOFC (piggy back) terminals but on a large layout there may be two or more facilities of the same type so cars can be shipped between points on the same layout.

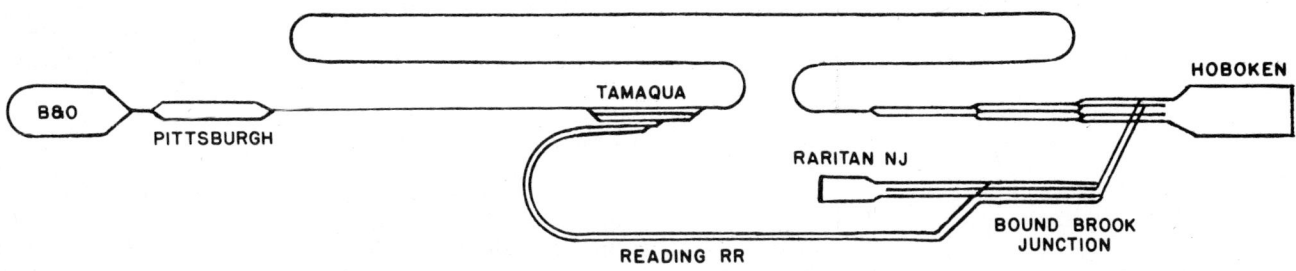

Fig. 10 Freight interchange concept

Chapter 2

CHAPTER 3
BENCHWORK

3.1 GENERAL

With the exception of specialized examples such as some portable layouts, outdoor railroads, or those built into furniture, model railroads are built on benchwork which, by definition, is the framework which supports the layout. No layout can be better than its supports; therefore the benchwork must be both strong and rigid for a reliable, trouble-free railroad. Strong because it is a virtual certainty that some one, perhaps more than one, will climb onto the benchwork. Rigid because the benchwork must not flex unduly under overloads even if it is strong enough to support them. Flexing of the benchwork applies strain on the track and scenery.

The benchwork design adopted will place limitations on the layout design. Since it is the railroad, not the benchwork, which is the objective, approach benchwork design with an open mind. A preconceived notion blindly followed may force unnecessary restrictions on the trackwork plan; eye-level benchwork makes large yards impractical. Experience has shown that once a benchwork design has been adopted, the layout normally conforms to it with but minor modifications to the benchwork plan. Do not settle on a specific benchwork design or method of construction until the various alternatives can be tested against the preliminary layout plans for best match.

Many factors, some of which are in direct conflict with others, should be considered before selecting a specific type of benchwork or a particular benchwork design. Examine each of the factors separately then the trade-offs among them. For example high benchwork provides easier access under the layout, low benchwork easier access to the top of the railroad.

3.2 ACCESS

Access to Track

Perhaps experience on a large layout over a considerable period of time is required before a model railroader can truly appreciate the need for easy access to each and every track. On a first layout it is tempting to install wide benchwork, duck-unders, and access openings. All these wear thin in time. True, such expedients do allow extra track but, in general, that extra track just is not worth the pain of reaching it. The soundest rule is that all tracks must be reachable from a normal access aisle and all tracks with any sort of complications such as switches must be within easy reach.

The maximum reachable working distance depends upon the height of the benchwork and that of the modeler. On a home layout a tall man might take advantage of his height but any layout to be operated by many should be designed on the basis of average height, perhaps a bit under. All figures and distances shown in this Handbook are based on a man 5'8" (1.73m) tall.

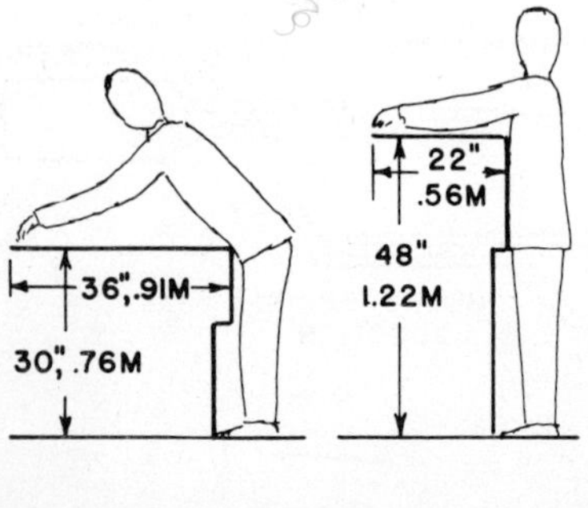

Fig. 1 shows the critical effect of benchwork height. On 30" (76cm) benchwork, tracks 36" (91cm) from the edge are reachable for maintenance but on 48" (122cm) high benchwork, the reachable distance is reduced to 22" (56cm).

View

Ability to see is important. As indicated in Fig. 2, benchwork 30" (76cm) high permits operation when seated yet when better viewing is required, the operator need only stand up. On high benchwork the operator must continually stand or sit on a high stool with no ready means for extending his view. Experience has shown that, on layouts with

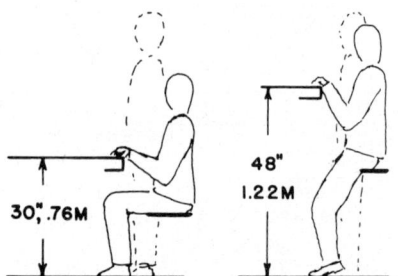

Fig. 2 Low benchwork permits a better view

low benchwork, most operators will stand during complex operations thus indicating that the best available view is often desired.

The justification given for high benchwork is that it provides a near eye-level view. That same type of view is had by a seated operator on low benchwork. When a modeler visits a prototype yard which has an overpass, he goes to that high vantage point. A better view is the reason the prototype places their operators in towers.

Layouts which are displayed to the public must consider viewing by children in selecting benchwork height. Although elevated viewing steps have been installed for use by children at public shows, they introduce a safety hazard.

Access for Operators and Visitors

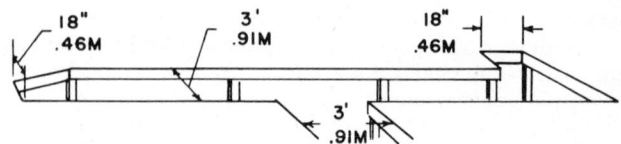

Fig. 3 Minimum aisle widths

There is a great temptation to reduce the width of access aisles to make more room for track. However it is important adequate space be provided for the free movement of operators and of visitors. Experience has shown that 2' (61cm) is about the narrowest aisle which can be considered reasonable but there will be interference when one operator attempts to pass another. 3' (91cm) aisles seem to be near optimum and allow free movement without extra space. Aisles used simultaneously both for visitors and for operators should be wider than 3' (91cm). The same applies to aisles with heavy traffic such as when walkaround control is installed.

Fig. 1 Reaching distance

A convenient method of keeping all track within easy reach of an aisle is the addition of short extensions to the main aisle. Since these extensions are used only for emergency work, they can be narrow, 18" (.46m) being adequate. Fig. 3 shows an access aisle and the minimum dimensions recommended in this Handbook.

Access Under Benchwork

Access to the underside of the layout is important but in no way as vital as convenient access to the top. Benchwork design should permit free movement under the layout. This means no braces or other projections which block passage. In general the space under the layout should not be used for storage but if it is, make the items under the benchwork easily movable, as by mounting them on wheels.

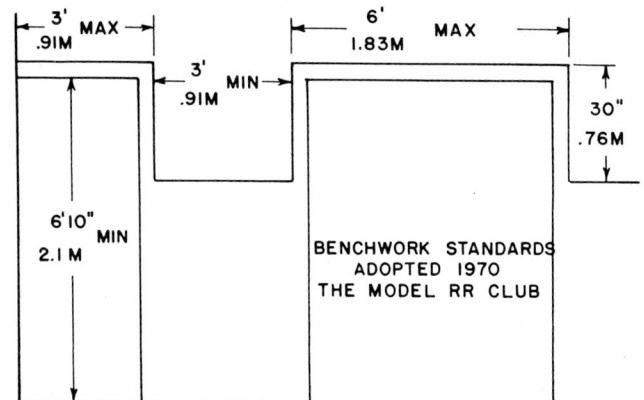
Fig. 6 Example of benchwork standards

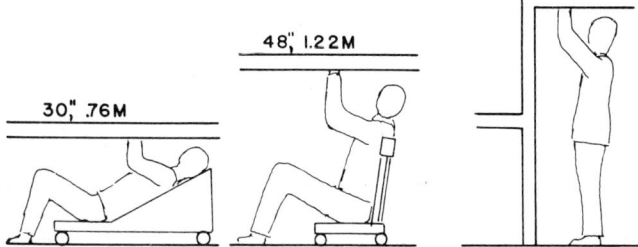
Fig. 4 Access under benchwork

The higher the benchwork, the better the access under it. Full headroom under the benchwork with elevated operating aisles as on the right in Fig. 4 is the ultimate in benchwork design from this standpoint. Unless full headroom exists, a carriage on casters is useful for working on the underside of the layout, where benchwork heights permit, some have mounted casters to the seat of a straight wooden chair as at the center of Fig. 4. Lower benchwork requires a more specialized reclining carriage. Fig. 5 is a photograph showing a skidder used under 30 " (.76m) high benchwork.

The benchwork standards of Fig. 6 guarantee that all tracks will be within 3' (.91m) of an access aisle except where two benchworks intersect as shown in Fig. 7. The cross-hatched areas in the figure are called forbidden zones at the club and the design rules permit exposed tracks to pass through such areas only if they contain no complications such as switches or crossings and are either straight or of a radius larger than the minimum. The forbidden zone on the left is of maximum size but such large zones are not permitted. The benchwork is always adjusted to reduce these zones to manageable sizes as indicated on the right, an actual case at that club.

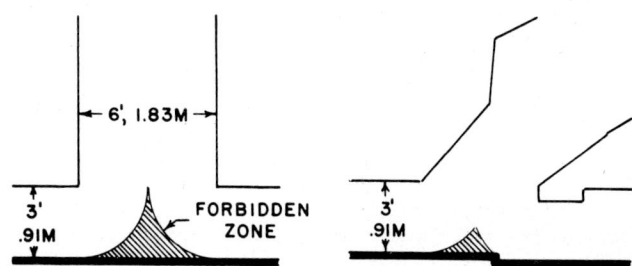
Fig. 7 Zones beyond standard maximum reach

3.3 BENCHWORK TYPES

Table-top or Grid Construction

Benchwork can have a flat top such as a piece of plywood as shown on the left in Fig. 8. This type of benchwork is called 'table top' and is used primarily for temporary or portable layouts (Section 3.72). Its large, flat surface acts as a sounding board and makes difficult the construction of tracks at different levels. In addition it cuts off access to the bottom of elevated tracks and to the scenery. Far superior to table top for most layouts is the grid or open-frame benchwork shown on the right. It is easy to fasten risers to support the track to the joists and the open construction permits access to the sub-roadbed and scenery.

Fig. 5 An underbenchwork skidder

Benchwork Standards

After the various factors have been considered, standards for benchwork should be adopted which guarantee adequate access. Once adopted, such standards should be followed scrupulously, not violated here and there for the sake of an extra track. Obviously standards will vary from layout to layout but as an illustration, Fig. 6 shows the benchwork standards adopted by The Model Railroad Club in 1970. These standards have particular weight as they represent the combined judgement of three clubs each with over 21 years of experience on distinctly different layouts with benchwork of various heights and widths.

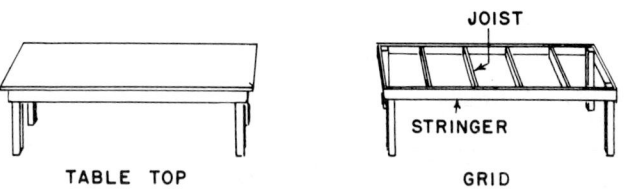
Fig. 8 Table-top and grid construction

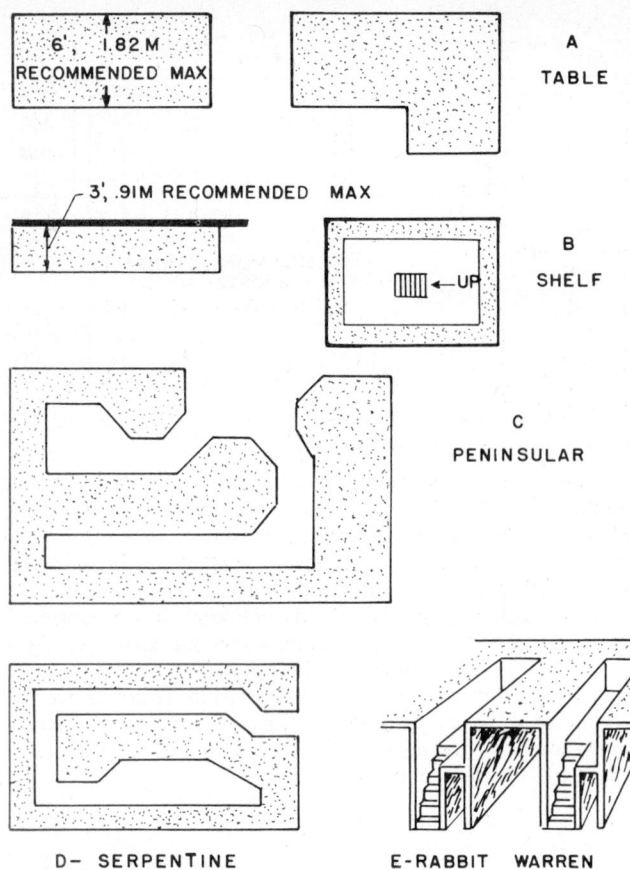

Fig. 9 Types of benchwork

section which has proved truly satisfactory over many years. A major problem is the changing length of the opening section itself and the relative movement of the benchwork on either side of the opening with time and changes of humidity. If opening benchwork must be installed, it is suggested they be made of metal rather than wood and the sides of the opening stabilized by metal. Some construction methods are covered in The Trackwork Handbook referenced in Section 6.1.

It is vital that opening sections be strong and well made with provision for being clamped in alignment when closed. Fig. 10 is a photograph of the more successful of two opening benchwork sections which were in service for many years at the Summit-New Providence HO RR Club, N.J. Posts from the concrete floor to the ceiling stabilized the ends of the benchwork opening. The gate itself was a sheet of plywood hinged to one post and, when closed, clamped to the other with a toggle clamp capable of exerting hundreds of pounds of force both top and bottom so all tracks would be forced into alignment. Vertical alignment was obtained at the free end by ball-bearing wheels being driven up a steel track. At public shows this gate was opened every few minutes as it spanned the visitor entrance to the layout room. Although it worked well when adjusted, it required adjustment many times each year. As a result of experience on this gate and the other which was in service even longer, the club ruled out gates on its second layout.

If a passage must be provided to an internal access aisle, a duck-under offers far more reliable operation than a movable section such as a gate. If the benchwork over the opening is kept both narrow and high as indicated in Fig. 11, it is not an unreasonable barrier to passage. It is suggested that such duck-unders be of substantial benchwork construction as shown rather than a scale bridge. This not only prevents damage but the benchwork can serve as a handy support to assist those no longer flexible in the knees. If there are several levels of track over a benchwork opening, the highest can be run as a duck-under which

Table, Shelf, Peninsular, Serpentine, Rabbit-Warren

Small layouts, particularly portable layouts, are often built as free-standing benchwork with access on all sides as shown at A in Fig. 9. Such benchwork is called 'table'. Do not confuse *table* benchwork, the shape, with *tabletop* benchwork, the construction (Fig. 8).

When the benchwork is against a wall, as at B in Fig. 9, it is called shelf benchwork. Since shelf benchwork cannot be wide for access reasons, unless the shelf extends completely around the room, loops are not practical except for small scales such as N or for short-radii lines such as traction.

Peninsular benchwork, Fig. 9, provides turning room and a continuous access without duck-unders or removable sections. The peninsulas can be used for terminals or other complex trackage (Fig. 24, Chapter 7) provided such tracks are not beyond easy reach from the aisles.

Benchwork with one long aisle, Fig. 9 D, is well suited for walkaround control. It is usually called serpentine.

Suitable only for rooms with adequate ceiling height is benchwork where the access aisles are interconnected by full headroom passages under the railroad as at E in Fig. 9. Suggested as early as 1951, this form of benchwork, called rabbit warren after John Armstrong, has seldom been used even though it places the least restrictions on layout design.

Small layouts may be completely of one type of benchwork but most large layouts are a combination of forms.

3.4 MOVABLE SECTIONS AND DUCK UNDERS

It is tempting to provide openings through the benchwork for passage, a typical case being at the entrance door to the room so tracks can be carried past the door. Such opening sections carrying tracks should be avoided if at all possible. The author has never seen an opening benchwork

Fig. 10 Access gate through benchwork

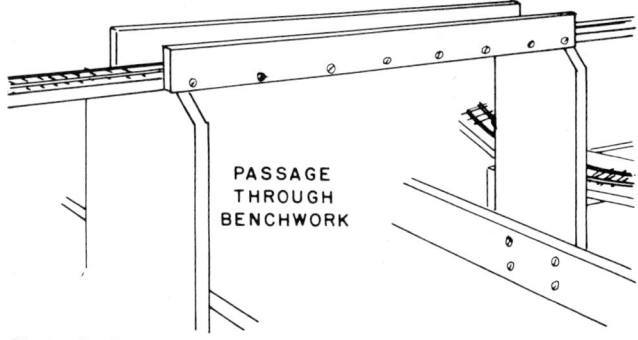

Fig. 11 Duck-under

will help stabilize the opening for a gate carrying the lower tracks. This was in fact done on the gate at the Summit-New Providence HO RR Club which gave access to the engineer cabs although originally the upper track was to have been mounted on the gate along with the other four tracks.

3.5 TWO-LEVEL AND HANGING BENCHWORK

Although seldom used, two-level benchwork provides more layout in the same floor space. Fig. 12 shows three different forms of two-level benchwork and one multi-level. At A is shown a form used for many years at the Summit-New Providence HO RR Club. The bottom level was divided by a backdrop into two separate scenes. The upper level was conventional. Since this section of benchwork was scenically independent of the rest of the layout, the tracks entered each level directly with no need to have an interconnection between levels.

At B is another form of two-level benchwork included in the plans of the same club but never built before the layout was abandoned in 1972. To avoid interference with the lower level, the upper level was to hang from the ceiling. At C is a form of two-level benchwork suggested by John Armstrong. The two-level floor may present a safety hazard but the author knows of no installation of this type. Where the benchwork must be narrow in any event, multiple-level benchwork as at D may be the way to a longer run of track. A home layout with two-level benchwork is shown in Fig. 8, Chapter 2. In that case the track climbs on the scenery of the lower level until the upper level is reached.

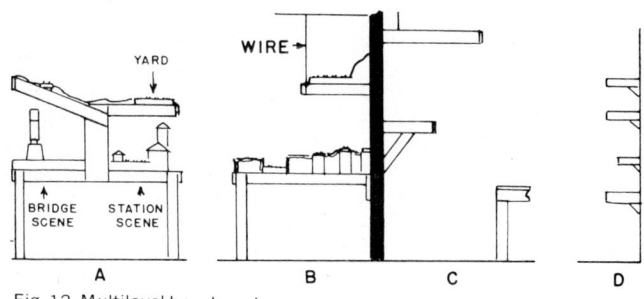

Fig. 12 Multilevel benchwork

3.6 SCENIC CONSIDERATIONS

The benchwork design should facilitate the installation of scenery (Chapter 4). Real railroads must provide for drainage which generally means ditches alongside the tracks with an occasional culvert through the roadbed. To provide the necessary room it is good practice to elevate the lowest track a minimum of 1½" (4cm) in N, 2" (5cm) in HO, or 3" (8cm) in O above the top of the benchwork proper as indicated in Fig. 13. One of the problems of table-top benchwork is that the lowest level of track normally is laid directly on the table top with no room for ditches.

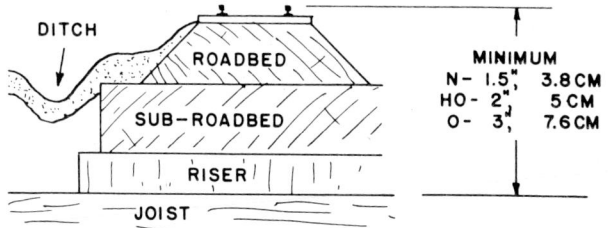

Fig. 13 Lowest track elevated above joist

For the sake of convenient access to the underside of the layout, the joists should be as high as is consistent with the scenery alongside the lowest track. Roads and streams passing under the lowest track usually can be placed between two joists so such features can be lower than the tops of the joists. When the depressed scenic feature is too large to be placed between joists, a wide ravine for example, a section of lowered benchwork can be installed as shown in Fig. 14. There is no reason why the entire benchwork has to be of uniform height.

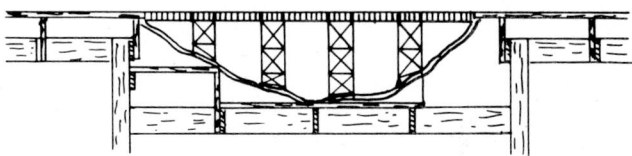

Fig. 14 Depressed benchwork

Most model railroaders build benchwork with horizontal joists but when steep mountains are being modeled it may be more convenient to tilt the joists to the approximate average angle of the scenery as shown on the left in Fig. 15. John Allen has demonstrated the spectacular effects which can be achieved by starting the scenery directly from the floor as on the right in the figure thus making the entire access aisle a canyon. Tilting the joists gives easier access to the upper levels of the tracks and scenery from underneath and reduces the length of the risers. Other tilted joists are shown in Fig. 12.

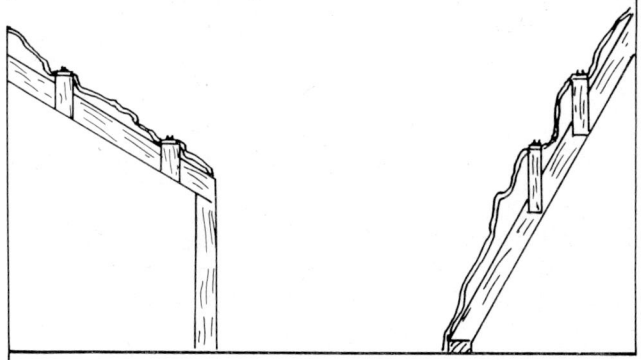

Fig. 15 Tilted joists

3.7 BENCHWORK CONSTRUCTION

3.71 General

Several different benchwork construction methods have proven satisfactory over the years. The selection of a particular method should be made only after all the requirements placed on the benchwork are known so the method most suitable for the layout contemplated is chosen. It is the railroad which is important, not the benchwork. The latter is only a means to the end.

Benchwork may be classified as portable, movable, or permanent. Portable means a layout designed to be transported frequently. The design of the benchwork for portable layouts is specialized and critical. Movable benchwork means it can be relocated but only with considerable effort, perhaps even including sawing the layout into sections. Permanent benchwork implies it can be moved only by being dismantled. Small layouts can easily be made movable but large layouts must have special construction and considerable limitations on the freedom of track design so they can be separated into handleable units. Unless it is likely that a layout must be moved in less than ten years, experience has shown the extra effort and the design restrictions caused by building movable benchwork rarely is productive. Seldom will new space be suitable for the old layout. Even more likely, advantage will be taken of moving after a long period of years to build a new layout to higher standards than the old.

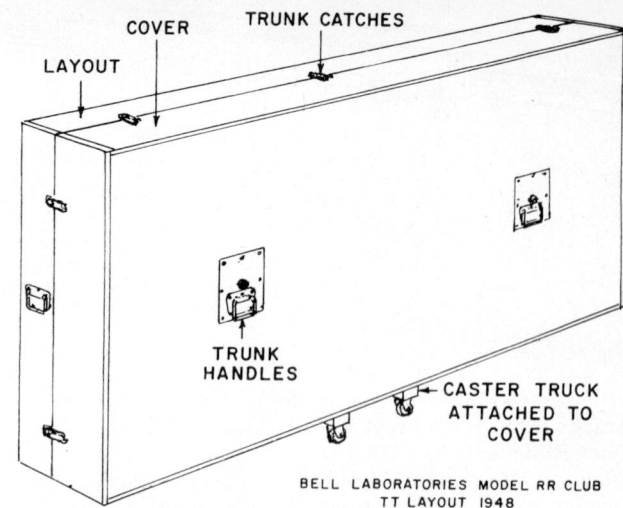

Fig. 17 Portable layout ready for shipment

It is recommended that portable layouts not be so large they cannot be in one piece. The layout shown in Figs. 16 to 18 is based on a 4'x8' (1.2 x 2.4m) sheet of plywood which probably is about as large as a single unit should be built for general use. If a portable layout must be built in sections, a strong, accurate means must be provided of aligning and fastening the sections together. Heavy loose-pin butt door hinges are effective for this purpose.

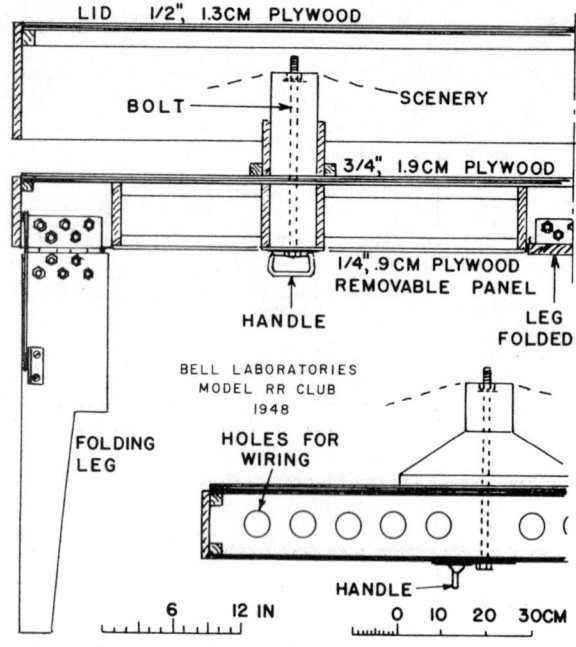

Fig. 16 Portable benchwork

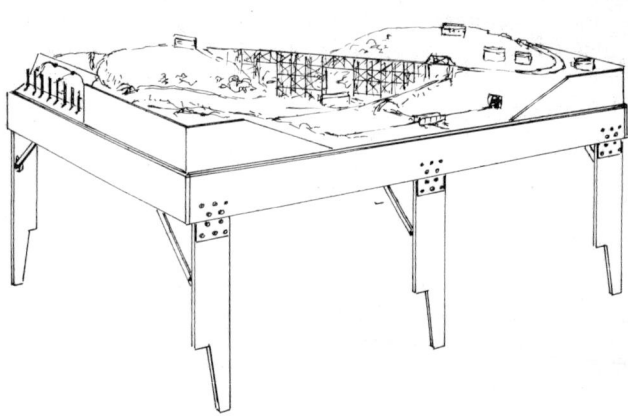

Fig. 18 Portable layout set up

3.72 Portable Benchwork

Portable benchwork must be much stronger than conventional benchwork including being able to resist twisting. Further, portable benchwork should protect the layout completely during shipments. The typical portable layout has a short life because of inadequate benchwork. An exception is one built in 1948 in TT scale, now converted to N, by the Bell Laboratories Model Railroad Club and still in excellent condition in 1976 after many long-distance shipments and frequent set ups and tear downs. The basic benchwork of that layout is a well-braced plywood box as shown in Fig. 16. For shipment a plywood cover is attached by means of the two through-bolts and heavy trunk-type fasteners along the edge. This top also has a built-on caster dolly for rolling the layout on its edge. The legs fold up to complete the shipping box. A drawing of this layout in its shipping condition is given in Fig. 17 and set up in Fig. 18. Fig. 9 of Chapter 4 shows this layout in operation. The two through bolts project out of hill tops and are covered by two pieces of removable scenery when the layout is open. Except for those two pieces and the rolling stock, the lid encloses everything so nothing else needs to be dismantled or removed for shipment. The important thing to note in the benchwork shown in Fig. 16 is that all hardware including the hinges, handles, and lid clamps are heavy duty. Also that all parts are well-fastened. Even the removable panels on the bottom are fastened with screws at frequent intervals as these panels add materially to the strength of the benchwork.

3.73 Permanent Benchwork

Most permanent benchworks are built as open grids. The joist spacings range from 12" (30cm) to 24" (60cm) as indicated in Fig. 19. Too close spacing makes it difficult to reach up between the joists and too large a spacing requires stronger than usual sub-roadbed.

The two most common forms of benchwork construction are shown in Fig. 19. That on the left, called conventional in this Handbook, has been used essentially since the beginning of model railroading. L (or T) girder construction as on the right was introduced by Linn Westcott in the Sept. 1963 Model Railroader and has become popular. With L girder construction the ends of the joists can be open and may project beyond the stringers as indicated thus reducing the need to duck under the benchwork. The clearance under the L-girder stringer is less than with conventional construction.

For permanent benchwork, advantage should be taken of every fixed support such as a buiding wall or column to stabilize the benchwork. One end of the joists can be supported by blocks nailed to the wall as indicated at the center left of Fig. 19. This is particularly suitable when the wall is of heavy construction such as a cinder-block cellar wall.

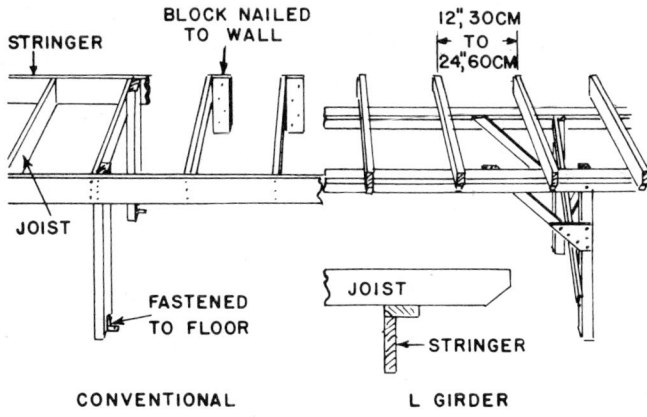

Fig. 19 Popular benchwork constructions

Hardened steel cut nails drive well into cinder block. Substantial support from the building plus fastening of the legs to the floor eliminates any special bracing thus giving maximum freedom of access under the layout. If the benchwork cannot be attached to the building, then the legs must be braced, one method being shown on the right in Fig. 19. A diagonal brace, not shown in Fig. 19, running horizontally under the joists is required to hold the benchwork square but this brace often can be removed after the sub-roadbed is in place.

Typically, permanent benchwork is assembled with flathead wood screws, No. 8 1½" (3.8cm) is a good size, or by nails such as 8 penny common. In all cases seen by the author screws were used to attach joists to L girders but nails have proven successful with conventional benchwork. For example in 1948 the Summit-New Providence HO RR Club nailed its benchwork together with the intention of adding screws but 25 years later when the benchwork was dismantled, the screws had never been added as the nails had done the job unaided.

Special conditions lead to special forms of benchwork. Roy Dohn, Montreal, when building a new home, had 2x4 benchwork joists built into his cellar walls so legs were unnecessary. Fig. 20 shows the rabbit-warren benchwork for the HO layout of The Model Railroad Club. All weight is carried wood to wood, the nails being used only to hold the members in alignment. Their N gauge railroad and O gauge switching line were built under the gambrels at balcony level and the benchwork takes maximum advantage of the building for its supports. Joists are spaced at 24" (61cm) on both types of benchwork.

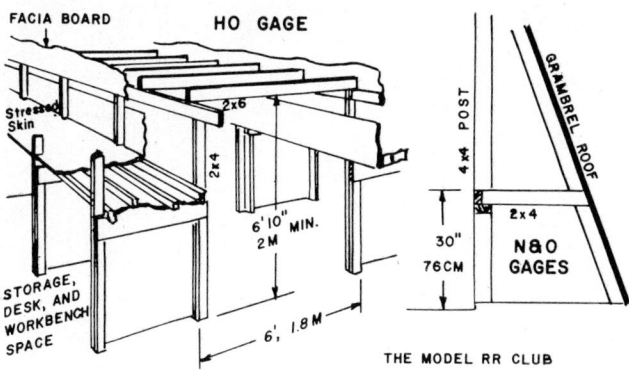

Fig. 20 Special benchworks

3.74 Movable Benchwork

Movable benchwork is similar in construction to free-standing permanent benchwork but stronger joints and extra bracing are required. Screws rather than nails should be used. The ease with which modern glues can be applied recommends the use of glue blocks to reinforce the joints. If more than one move can be anticipated, legs should be bolted on rather than screwed. Fig. 21 is an example of movable benchwork construction.

Layouts too large to move in one piece should be designed with convenient separation points to divide it into handleable units. A minimum number of tracks should cross such division points and as nearly at right angles as is feasible.

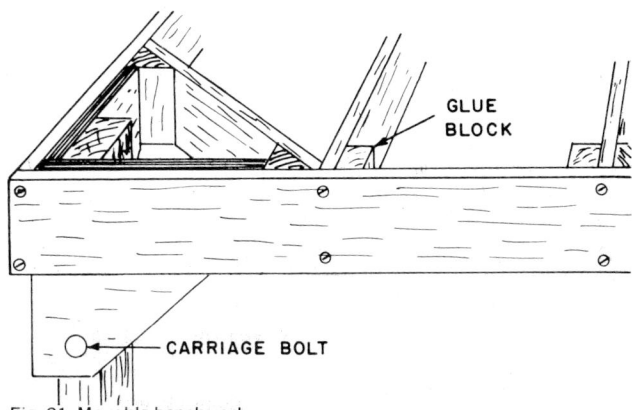

Fig. 21 Movable benchwork

When more than one move is expected, it is advisable to build the benchwork as separate units bolted together, one method being shown in Fig. 21 for L girder construction. Accurate alignment devices are not needed as care can be taken when reassembling the benchwork. However it assists if drivefit holes for rods or heavy nails are drilled through the mating parts before disassembly. Rods driven through these holes when reassembling the benchwork will guarantee the original alignments.

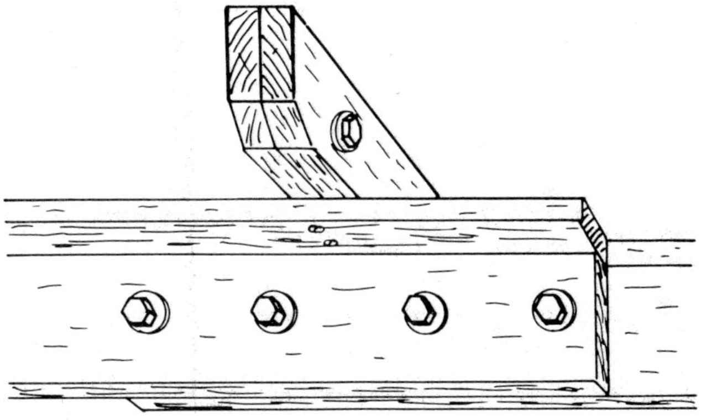

Fig. 22 Bolted splice in L-Girder construction

Rather than attempting to place rail joiners at precisely the correct location for dividing the layout, more reliable operation is likely if a foot or so of the track is relaid over the dividing point after the layout has been reassembled.

When not more than one move is likely, consideration should be given to building the benchwork without a break but with designed locations for divisions where the benchwork can be cut into units as shown in Fig. 23. To reassemble, splice blocks are screwed and glued to all cut members as indicated by the dotted lines in the figure.

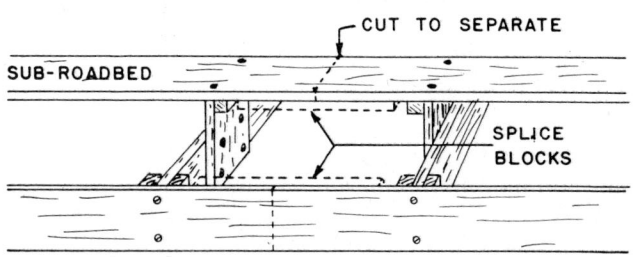

Fig. 23 Disassembly by cutting

Chapter 4
BASIC SCENERY

4.1 GENERAL

No stage of layout design should ever be divorced from scenery considerations, not even the first steps of choosing the concept of the railroad. The assumed geographical location and the types of towns served have a profound effect upon the scenery. As plans progress the scenery becomes more and more detailed, for example how to conceal curving tracks at room corners. Finally the exact plans for buildings are selected or the particular rock formations chosen. The last-named final details are outside the scope of a handbook on design but can be found in the various books on scenery.

4.2 OVERALL SCENERY

As described in Chapter 2, one of the objectives served by the concept for the railroad is the provision of a guide for realistic scenery. Obviously the structures, the vegetation, and many other items are quite different for a mining town in Nevada as compared with a small industrial town in Ohio.

A small layout is restricted in the variety of scenery which can be included. It is far more realistic to model a single location well than to attempt a melange. A large layout can change from one type of scenery to another in a reasonable distance without upsetting the visual effect.

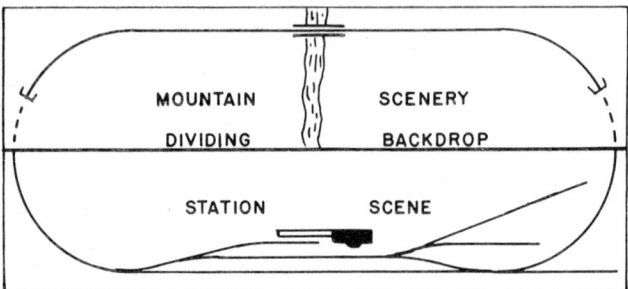

Fig. 1 Dividing backdrop

One method of permitting distinctly different scenes to be included even on a small layout is the use of a scenery backdrop. As an example Fig. 1 shows a small OO layout planned and partially built by the author in 1934. A dividing backdrop separated the station area which was designed for operation from a mountain scene. The track in the mountains served to display moving trains but operationally merely permitted a train departing to the west to return to the station as an arriving train from the east. Another example of this type of dividing backdrop is shown in Fig. 12A, Chapter 3.

Dividing backdrops running parallel to the aisle are particularly well suited to layouts with walkaround control as the engineer is with his train and it is not important that the backdrop blocks his view of other parts of the layout. John Armstrong made extensive use of such dividing backdrops on his layout.

Optical dividers can be across the benchwork as well as along it. Fig. 2 shows how a relatively small shelf railroad could be divided to permit radically different scenes to be included. The new layout (1973) of the Rensselaer Model RR Society, N.Y., made particularly extensive use of both longitudinal and across the benchwork dividers (Fig. 17).

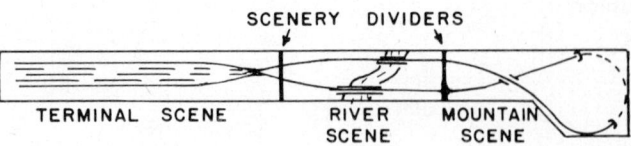

Fig. 2 Scenery dividers

When there is more than one station on the layout, it makes for greater interest if each has its own particular characteristic. Do not wait until plans have progressed to some tentative tracks at each station before settling on the type of station. Rather select the basic concept for the station at the very beginning. Tracks for an industrial district are quite different than those serving a rural community.

Even on a large layout it is generally impractical to duplicate all the trackwork at a given prototype station although there are successful examples of this being done, for example a home layout in Watertown, N.Y. had a complete scale replica of the entire Watertown station. Seldom, however, are the points of interest so concentrated or physically so small that they can be modeled to full scale size with scale intervening distances. Selective compression usually must be employed. This means retaining the features in a recognizable form so the flavor of the particular prototype area is retained. The station, if large, can be compressed and distinctive buildings moved closer to the tracks yet remain recognizable. Visitors are always more impressed by a layout if they can identify it with the real thing Anyone who saw the O scale representation of the Delaware Water Gap on the layout of the New York Society of Model Engineers in the Lackawanna Terminal at Hoboken, N.J. will never forget it. It was an impressive sight and immediately recognizable although much compressed over the prototype.

The late John Allen successfully compressed many different scenes one next to the other on his Gorre & Daphetid, a fact which surprised visitors who had previously known his HO layout only by means of photographs.

4.3 BENCHWORK CORNERS

Except for layouts arranged as in Fig. 2, model railroads are faced with a succession of corners. Some prototype curves exist without a visible reason, perhaps due to the land which could be purchased for right of way, so not all model curves must have an obvious reason. Most prototype curves, however, have some apparent cause, a bend in the river, a mountain, or even a minor change in elevation of the land. In general it is best if the scenery on a model railroad either provides a reason for the 90 degree curve necessary at a corner or hides that turn.

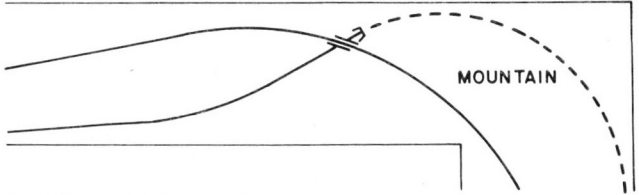

Fig. 3 A mountain to conceal a corner

Fig. 3 shows two methods of using a mountain at a benchwork corner. The upper track is obviously turning due to the shape of the mountain. The lower track appears to be tunneling through the mountain range rather than curving with the upper track. See also the mirror method of Fig. 23.

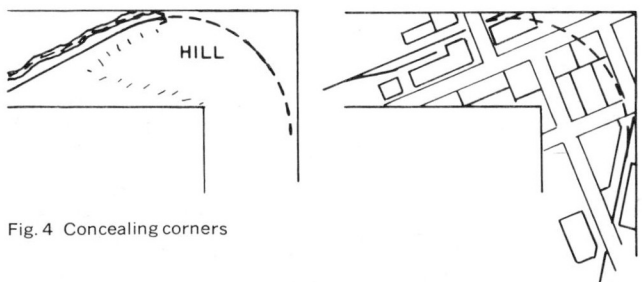

Fig. 4 Concealing corners

An effective way of hiding a curve is to build the track so it appears to be following a stream coming in from the backdrop as shown on the left in Fig. 4. The scenery should be arranged so that the tunnel portal is not visible from any normal viewing angle. Other types of scenery can be used with this same technique. On the right in Fig. 4 the scenery has been arranged so that the railroad appears to be two different lines heading for a grade crossing beyond the walls. The buildings should be located and of such a character it is quite obvious that a right of way is extending between them. The scenery should conceal the start of the curve from all normal viewing angles or, alternatively, the actual line could appear as a spur leading into one of the buildings.

Roger Ramsdell used a covered bridge on his O scale layout as shown in Fig. 5. The track curving out from the rear of the bridge was concealed quite well by trees on a small rise. Fig. 6 is a photograph of his bridge.

Mirrors are another means of camouflaging a corner. One method is to build a false main line perpendicular to a mirror as shown in Fig. 7. The scenery should be arranged to permit the reflected continuation of the line to be readily

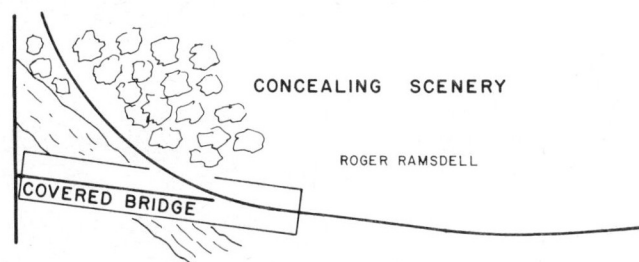

Fig. 5 Covered bridge conceals curve

Fig. 6 Covered bridge on the O gauge Rockland RR, by Roger Ramsdell

visible. The actual curving route could appear as the end of a spur, or, if the mirror reflects a grade crossing as on the right in Fig. 7, the actual route would appear as an interchange track. If the track is concealed but its reflection is not, the track can appear to leave the benchwork (Fig. 23). A mirror is far superior to any backdrop scene when extending foreground as what is real and what is reflected are virtually indistinguishable thus doubling the scenery area as far as effect is concerned (Section 4.7).

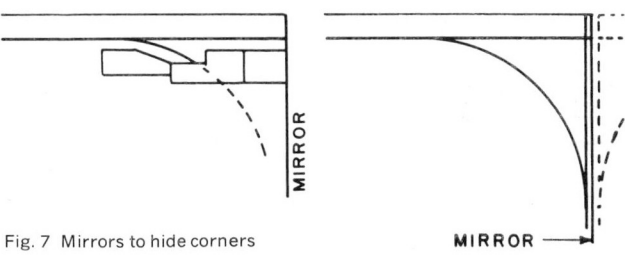

Fig. 7 Mirrors to hide corners

4.4 RIVERS AND STREAMS

The general location of major rivers and streams should be part of the original concept. Since streams are not constrained by minimum radius or maximum grades, their locations can be adjusted to suit the track pattern. Nevertheless it is important that space for waterways be considered at all stages of planning, otherwise it may be difficult to squeeze anything other than drainage ditches and brooks in among the tracks.

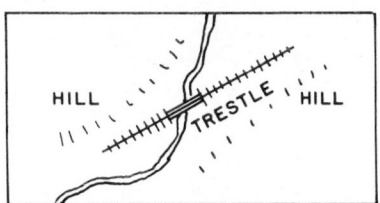

Fig. 8 Stream on a small layout

Fig. 9 TT gauge portable layout

Chapter 4

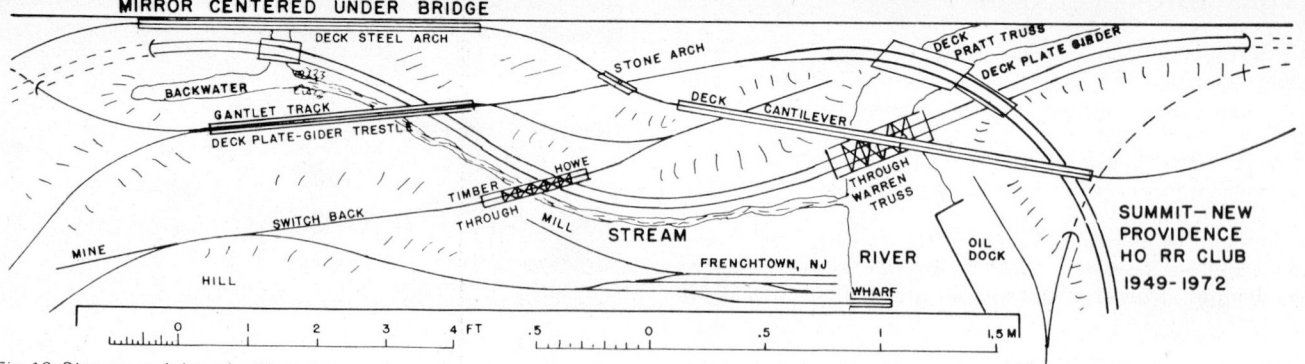

Fig. 10 Streams and rivers justify routes

Even the smallest layouts can feature a sizable stream. The initial concept for a small layout might be formed around the longest and highest trestle which can be placed on the benchwork available as in Fig. 8. This was the concept of the layout built on the benchwork shown in Fig. 16, Chapter 3. The trestle was built of brass by H. J. Braun and is shown in Fig. 9.

In Fig. 8 the stream was used to justify a trestle crossing the valley of that stream but railroads also follow waterways as on the left in Fig. 4 in addition to crossing them. Fig. 10 shows this concept as it was being implemented at the time the first layout of the Summit-New Providence HO RR Club was abandoned in 1972. The double-track followed the course of the small stream at the bottom of a gorge. A mirror was used to extend this stream visually through the wall, the backwater in the foreground appearing as the continuation of the stream in the reflection, the actual extension of the stream was to be concealed by vegetation in the reflection. Half a steel arch bridge 5' (1.5m) long was built against the mirror, a space-saving way of building a major bridge. The hill in the foreground prevented viewers from seeing themselves in the mirror.

The larger river in Fig. 10 provided justification for major bridges including a cantilever 6' (1.8m) long. Since larger streams can be navigable, a barge-to-tank car transfer point was installed on one side of the river and a wharf served by the traction line was projected on the other.

Note in Fig. 10 that the bridges were of distinctly different types. The bridge on the double-track line in front of the mirror was planned as a plate girder on one side and a concrete arch on the other so the reflected bridge would be quite different from the direct-view bridge.

Rivers make excellent dividers. Fig. 11 shows a navigable river included in the plans of an HO layout. The river separates the passenger station at Newark from the freight yard at Harrison, also the passenger station at Easton from the freight yard at Phillipsburg. These situations were based on prototype railroad crossings of the Passaic and the Delaware Rivers respectively.

Although useful to justify track routings or a featured structure such as the long trestle of Fig. 8, rivers are an attractive and interesting feature in their own right. An example is Fig. 12 which shows a portion of the now-dismantled layout of the Wolverine Model Railroad Club in Detroit. Note the spaciousness around the bridge in the photograph, typical of real railroad river crossings. Such an attractive setting can only be obtained if the river is planned at an early stage and not just slipped in between tracks. Particularly if the water level is well below the tracks, consider rivers when planning the benchwork. A dropped benchwork section as shown in Fig. 14, Chapter 3 might be necessary for the best effect.

In cramped quarters, such as in an industrial area, a canal rather than a river might be a better choice. Canal banks are usually much more regular in shape than those of a river and the waterway is narrower than a navigable river. A canal introduces the opportunity to construct one, perhaps several, interesting small movable bridges. Railroad-to-barge transfer points add operational interest. Fig. 13 shows an HO industrial area with a canal which was under construction in 1974.

Fig. 12 River scene at the Wolverine Model RR Club

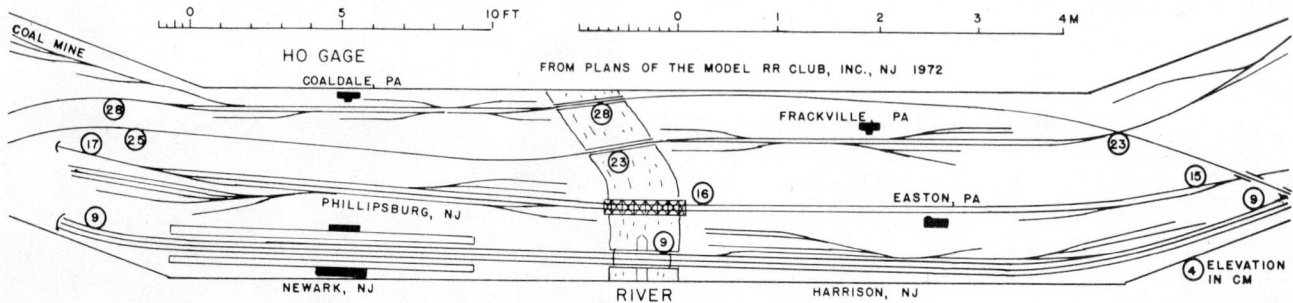

Fig. 11 Rivers serve as scenery dividers

16 Chapter 4

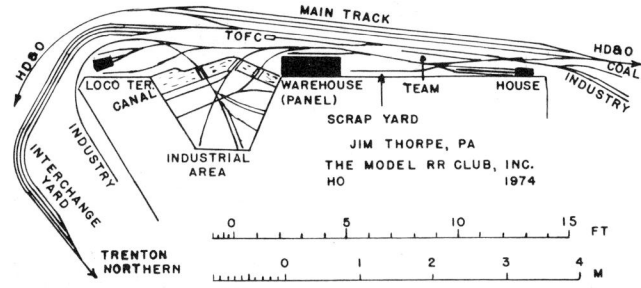

Fig. 13 Industrial area with canal

4.5 DRAINAGE

Drainage encompasses the ditches and minor streams which carry away water runoff from rain. Consider a heavy rain falling on the scenery. Where would the water run? In particular look for places where the water would be dammed by the railroad. On the prototype there are numerous culverts (openings through the roadbed) to carry water from the uphill side of the track to the downhill side. Although most model railroads have at least one bridge, culverts are seldom modeled but should be.

Fig. 14 Culvert

Fig. 14 shows an application of a culvert to drain a large watershed on one side of the track. There is no reason why water need be modeled in such culverts and ditches. Many such ditches are dry except after a rain.

Because of their small size, ditches and culverts are often thought of as scenery details which can be added at the time the layout is built. To a large extent this is true. Nevertheless it facilitates such later installation if the general requirements of drainage are considered during the planning phases (Fig. 2, Chapter 9).

The other side of the coin is that where there is a drainage ditch on a model, there should be some apparent source of water. The author has seen a rather well-done dry drainage ditch modeled down the side of a fill. Unfortunately there was no apparent source of water to justify such a ditch.

4.6 PLANNED CONSTRUCTION SEQUENCE

On a small layout, say 5' by 9' (1.5 by 2.7m), it is best to lay all track, wire and test for good operation before installing scenery. Large layout construction may progress for years, indeed may never be completed. On such railroads the layout plan should be designed so that the first stations and tracks to be built are those furthest from the aisles. Then these first tracks can be laid, wired, tested, and surrounded with scenery. This gives a finished look to the operating part of the railroad without risking damage to that scenery during later construction. The greatest mistake made by the Summit-New Providence HO RR Club, N.J. when it started construction in 1949 was to build the tracks nearest the aisles first. All scenery built along such tracks was either damaged or destroyed when tracks to the rear were constructed later. Profiting from that experience, The Model Railroad Club designed its layout so the tracks against the wall (or the center tracks in the case of benchwork with aisles on both sides) were the first to be built. The plans called for placing hard-shell scenery on both sides of the completed tracks. Fig. 15 shows this planned sequence at one point on their layout.

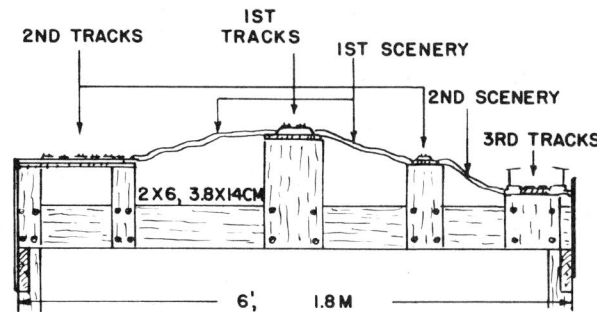

Fig. 15 Order of construction

4.7 BACKDROPS AND MIRRORS

General

Wherever benchwork ends against or near a wall, a backdrop or mirror can be used to good effect to give an illusion of greater space. Both also can be used as scenery dividers. Backdrops are most often used to give the effect of far distances beyond the modeled scenery, mirrors to multiply the effect of the modeled scenery in front of the mirror. Effective use of backdrops is more a matter of scenery detail and skillful application than of layout design but their requirements should be kept in mind through all phases of design. Mirrors have many possibilities which can be exploited by the designer but they are at their best when included in the plans and not left as a finishing detail.

Backdrops

If the viewing angle is essentially fixed as is customary with a diorama and in photographs, it is possible to blend the modeled foreground scenery into a painted, printed, or photographic backdrop, even to use foreshortened models to give a greater feeling of depth. In most cases, however, model railroads are viewed from many angles which makes a direct connection between foreground and backdrop difficult as illustrated in Fig. 16. At A a road has been extended onto the backdrop. When viewed from the front the appearance is realistic but when viewed at an angle as at B, the change from the horizontal to the vertical is all too obvious. When a feature such as a road extends directly onto a

Typically northeastern granite rock outcroppings are well executed on The Model Railroad Club HO layout; blend skillfully into the painted backdrop. Photos and first hand knowledge of real rock makes it easier to model the scene in miniature.

backdrop it is better if the junction is concealed except when viewing from the designed angle. A solution is shown at C where an angle view of the junction of the scenery road and the background road is blocked by a building on one side and trees on the other. Buildings can butt directly against the backdrop. This is better than terminating a short distance away for it prevents the casting of an unrealistic shadow on the backdrop.

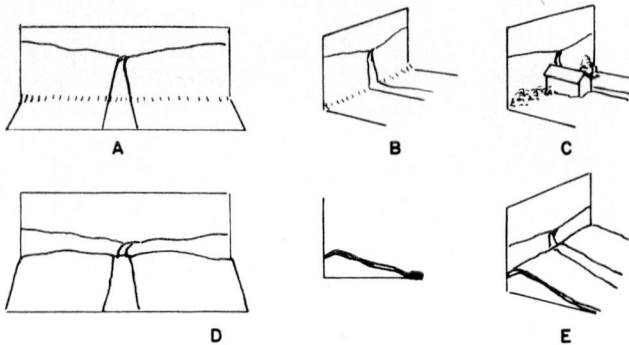

Fig. 16 Extending roads into backdrops

A building should not have an extension painted on the backdrop. The perspective of the modeled building will change with viewing angle, that of the painted building will remain the same. For the same reason nearby buildings should not be placed on the backdrop, say in an attempt to extend a city block. This is the same problem as demonstrated at B for the road. A similar problem exists with foreshortened buildings. They only look realistic when viewed from the designed angle of foreshortening. However scenery with no hard lines, such as the vegetation shown on the left at C in Fig. 16, can readily be carried over from model to backdrop.

Excellent results are obtained by cresting the modeled scenery an inch or so in front of the backdrop and painting a distant scene on the latter as at D. With the junction of backdrop and foreground out of sight, changing viewing angle has little effect as illustrated at E.

As a general rule the more distant from the viewers the backdrop scene, the more effective and easier to make it becomes. The El Paso Model Railroad Club had in the rear of its layout a plastered brick wall on which the lower part of the plaster had fallen away leaving a ragged lower edge. The club painted the plaster as sky, used its lower edge as the top of a mountain range and daubed hazy colors over the bricks. The author found this simple backdrop most impressive.

Backdrops can also be used to divide benchwork for different scenes as in Figs. 1 and 2, also Fig. 12, Chapter 3. Fig. 1, Chapter 8, shows a backdrop for the purposes of concealing a holding yard. Fig. 17 is taken from the plans of the Rensselaer Model RR Society, Troy, NY showing their proposed use of backdrops to separate scenery, conceal pipes, and to hide the loop effect at the end of a peninsula on their HO New England, Berkshire & Western.

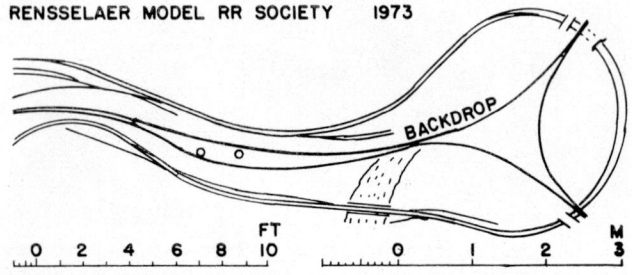

Fig. 17 Dividing backdrops

Mirrors

In contrast to backdrops which are best used to create the illusion of long distances but which are difficult to associate with foreground scenery, mirrors extend the foreground directly and the reflected image remains in true perspective regardless of viewing angle. For example the Summit-New Providence HO RR Club installed 15' of mirror along one wall, the mirror being at the center line of a street. Thus the 4' wide town to be modeled on the benchwork visually became twice that. Mirrors, however, do not provide the illusion of far distances, unless the reflected scene is of great depth as when John Allen used a mirror to reflect the entire length of his layout. (Fig. 15, Chapter 11.)

When mirrors, particularly small ones, are installed, best results are obtained if the mirror edges are concealed. A deck bridge at the rear of the benchwork is the most obvious application. One is shown in Fig. 10 and another in Fig. 18. In such a case the bridge serves as a frame for the mirror.

The reflected scene should appear to be different than the direct scene. Fortunately this usually is easily accomplished. The ten-span concrete arch trestle of Fig. 18 is an example. The stream makes a bend so vegetation on its banks can conceal the foreground tracks. This concealing barrier is extended by the material in a storage yard and by

Fig. 18 Mirrors under bridge

a building. The road opens into a parking lot in the foreground but the parking lot's reflection is blocked by the piers so its reflected image appears to be a road coming in from around a pier.

When a bridge or similar structure is near or against a wall as is the case in Fig. 18, mirrors not only extend the foreground through and beyond the structure but also provide proper illumination. If the scenery were carried through the arches in Fig. 18 to a backdrop, such a scenery extension would be in shadow.

The O gauge Madison, N.J. club installed a mirror under a high arch bridge to conceal an access opening behind the bridge.

Tracks leading directly to a mirror must reach it at right angles or with some symmetrical pattern. Fig. 19 presents three examples actually built with the reflected rails shown by dashed lines.

When the roof of a building can be seen, rectangular buildings must be set parallel or perpendicular to the mirror as at A in Fig. 20. Square or L-shaped buildings can be set at 45° as at B. Buildings at intersections often do not have parallel walls and lend themselves well to the mirror technique as at C. If the roof is above eye level, the wall can reach the mirror at any angle provided the reflection of that wall cannot be seen in the mirror and the wall which the viewer assumes is extending into the mirror could not be seen even if it existed.

With rear-silvered mirrors there is always a gap caused by the thickness of the glass. Therefore thin mirrors are best. The mirrors behind the bridge in Fig. 18 were the 1' squares used to make mirror walls. Such mirrors in 1974 were both thin and economical. Dark colored structures minimize the effect of the gap. Regardless of color, the same color as the outside walls or structural members should be placed on the surface flush against the mirror. Front-surfaced mirrors would eliminate this gap but such mirrors are expensive and their life questionable.

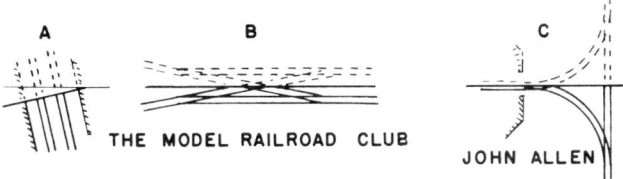

Fig. 19 Tracks against mirrors

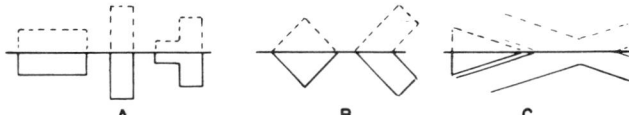

Fig. 20 Buildings against mirrors

Mirrors also can be used effectively to reflect scenery to one side and for multiple reflections to build distances in limited space. At A in Fig. 21 is the two-mirror method used by John Allen to create a long rapid-transit platform. He also created and filled with cars what appeared to be a large underground garage by this method. With two mirrors set at 120° John Allen built the apparent wye around storage tanks shown at B. The Sacramento Model RR Club installed a 45° mirror to create the illusion of a long street extending into the background as shown at C. The upper edge of the mirror was concealed by a banner over the street. Two mirrors at 90° were used by The Model RR Club to quadruple the size of a commercial district as indicated at D. A photograph of this particular installation appears in Fig. 22.

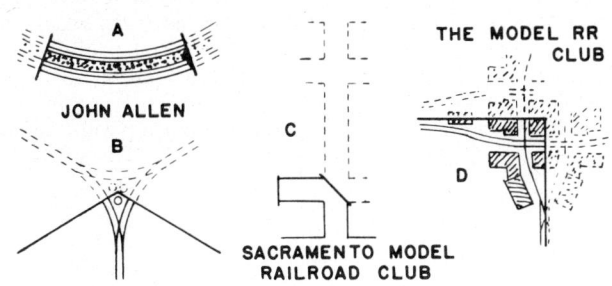

Fig. 21 Multiple mirrors

When the layout is primarily viewed from one side, it is possible to make the trains appear to go beyond the limits of the benchwork. Lorne Dean used a mirror as shown in Fig. 23A so the trains apparently turned in the opposite direction from their actual route. It is necessary that the scenery create a concealed zone as indicated. It may prove easier to create such a concealed zone by placing the mirror at an angle, 45° being shown at B in the figure.

Bridges are ideal for construction over a mirror but, if built against a mirror extending above the rails, bridges will appear to have at least two tracks. Customary prototype bridge construction does not provide a logical reason for screening the reflected image of a train crossing the bridge. If the bridge is at or above eyelevel, the reflected image of the train becomes much less noticeable. If a three-track

Fig. 22 Expanding an area with two mirrors

bridge is modeled (1½ real, 1½ reflected) a standing train could be modeled on the center track against the mirror thereby completely screening the reflection of the moving train.

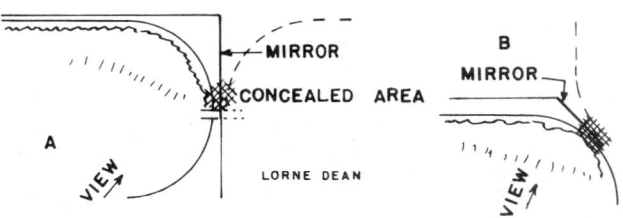

Fig. 23 Apparent tracks leaving benchwork

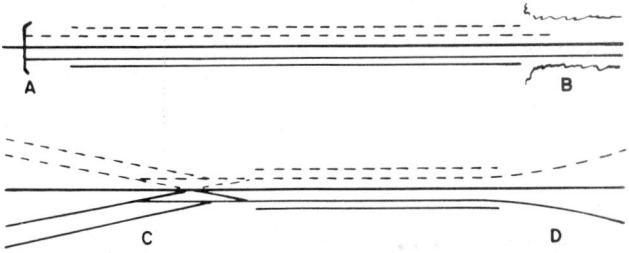

Fig. 24 Ending reflected tracks

The reflected tracks must have some logical termination. Fig. 24 shows four possibilities. At A the two tracks enter a tunnel. At B they disappear behind scenery. At C a junction is modeled which actually connects a double-track approach to a single track over the bridge. At D the two tracks simply diverge as separate single-track lines as in a prototype example in New Orleans.

Small mirrors often can be designed to be set at an angle or with a small rise in the foreground scenery to prevent the viewer from seeing himself. When that cannot be done, the effect is the same as another aisle on the other side of the scenery.

Mirrors also can be designed into the layout as operating aides, usually to permit the engineers to see around some obstruction. Scenery mirrors, strategically placed, can be used for the same purpose. The mirror under the bridge in Fig. 10 gave the engineers a view of a grade crossing (not shown) which was concealed from their direct view.

Most model railroads with mirrors use them on a small scale only, but there are exceptions, that of John Allen being noted earlier. When the Model RR Club extends their HO layout room to its ultimate length of 150' (48.8m), their plans, as of 1978, call for making the entire end wall a mirror against which will be built a scale model of the Quebec through cantilever Bridge (Fig. 23, Chapter 7). Thus from a viewing balcony at one end of the room the visitors will see an apparent 320' (97.5m) of layout with a huge bridge spanning the center. The mirror will also serve other purposes such as doubling the length of the yard at the Raritan terminal.

Chapter 4   19

CHAPTER 5
Electrical and Control

5.1 GENERAL

Electrical factors, particularly the method of control, have great impact on the design of all but the smallest layouts. Electrical problems, such as those posed by reversing loops, can always be solved at the expense of more complex circuits regardless of track design. Often, however, a inconsequential change in the track plan may completely eliminate the need for special circuits or at least permit circuits to be simplified. Therefore electrical requirements should be kept in mind so problem areas will be recognized.

The control system adopted normally places restrictions on layout design (Section 5-2). It is conceivable that a modeler is interested primarily in the electrical circuits with the layout serving as a showpiece for the controls. More often the wiring and controls are a means of making the railroad operate, not an end in themselves. If so, it is important that the control system adopted be the one best suited to the layout. A preconceived idea that a particular control system must be used may well reduce design opportunities and eliminate interesting possibilities. Walkaround control in particular places severe restrictions on layout design. Unless the layout is for the controls, examine the various control systems for the one most suitable for the layout.

The details of wiring, circuits, and control systems are outside the scope of this Handbook but may be found in the Electrical Handbook for Model Railroads by the same author and publisher as this Handbook.

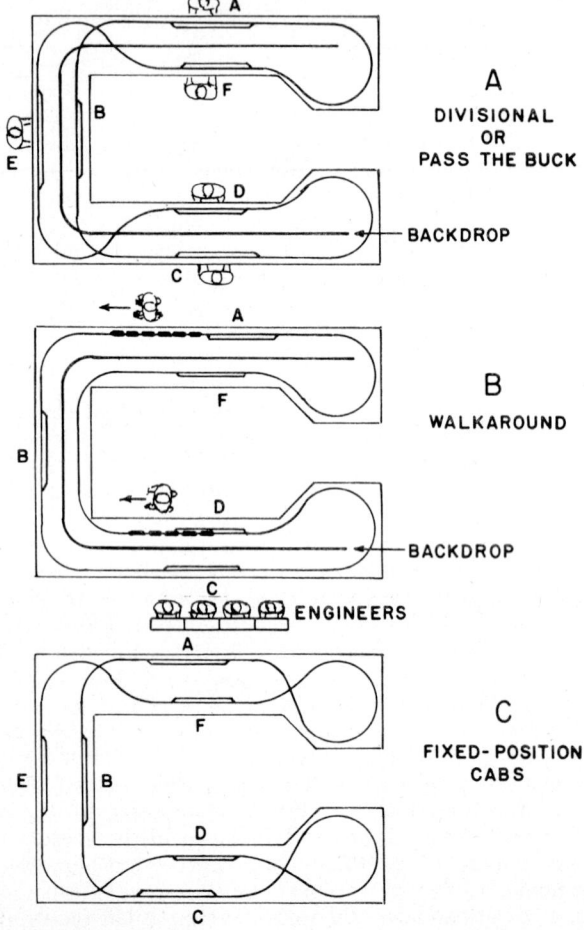

Fig. 1 Types of control

5.2 CONTROL SYSTEMS

For the purposes of layout design, control systems may be divided into three groups: divisional, walkaround, and fixed-position cabs (the latter commonly called simply cab control). These three systems are not mutually exclusive, any two or all three could be installed on the same layout. The differences among the systems as far as layout design is concerned lie in the requirements of access and visibility. Fortunately the restrictions imposed by each form do not interfere with either of the other two types of control. For example the type of access aisle required by walkaround control is equally suitable for divisional or fixed-cab control.

Division Control

With division control, also called pass-the-buck or sectional control, there are two or more operators each controlling a specific part of the railroad and operating all trains in that area. Each operator needs physical access and view only of the tracks he controls. As shown in Fig. 1 A, dividing backdrops may be used and the tracks between stations need not follow an aisle. This system of control places the least restrictions on layout design and for years was the most popular system. Unfortunately pass-the-buck, as that name implies, lacks continuity of control of each train, a hallmark of prototype operation. Therefore on layouts intended to be operated in the prototype manner, divisional control has been all superseded by systems in which an engineer controls a train for the duration of its run.

Walkaround Control

With walkaround control an engineer physically follows his train as it moves along the route. Electrically a great variety of systems can be used but all require that the engineer be able to walk alongside his train and have physical access and sight of that portion of the railroad as indicated in Fig. 1 B. Dividing backdrops can be used but the track must generally follow the aisles. See Fig. 17, Chapter 4 for an example of layout design for walkaround control.

Fixed-Position Cab Control

A prevalent control system in 1976 was to operate each train from controls mounted at a fixed position and called a cab. The engineer must be able to see his locomotive from his position at the cab regardless of the position of the locomotive on its route. Consequently dividing backdrops or other obstructions to his view cannot be used to any great extent but there is no constraint on the location of tracks with respect to the aisles as shown in Fig. 1 C. Where possible it is advantageous to elevate the cabs.

The engineers on a small layout usually not only can assist each other in the event a train derails or other manual operation is required but also they generally set the track route and perform functions assigned to several types of railroad employees. On large layouts the engineers at fixed-position cabs may be too remote from their train for such manual assistance or it may be desired to have station agents, towermen, and the like in the manner of the prototype. Such other operators may also be involved in setting up the electrical connection between the engineer cab and the locomotive. In any event the layout design must provide the necessary physical access to the track by such operators and also give them the necessary freedom of movement. Further, space for the control panels must be included at an early stage in the design. If deferred until after the tracks are drawn, it may be difficult to make room. However some model railroaders have found control panels suspended above the layout to be excellent, some believe superior to panels on the benchwork (Section 5.8).

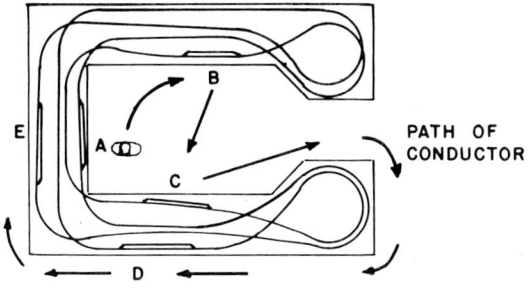

Fig. 2 Movement of a conductor

On some model railroads the engineer remains at a fixed cab but a conductor or brakeman follows the train to handle waybills and to give hand signals to the engineer when drilling. Although the layout design must provide for the movement of the conductor from station to station, he need not follow the route of the train as can be seen in Fig. 2.

The distinctions among forms of control become less and less with decreasing size and on the smallest layouts it often is impossible to say which system is in use.

5.3 REVERSING LOOPS AND WYES

Reversing loops are the delight of the beginner as they allow trains to dash hither and yon and come back the other way over a series of alternate routes. Such operation hardly models that of the prototype, rather it is more of a game. Reversing loops on the prototype have a specific purpose in each case. The loop at Bay Head Junction terminal of the New York and Long Branch is used to reverse passenger trains for their run back to New York City. The loops at Grand Central Terminal, NY were primarily an escape for the locomotives. Other loops are used for turning piggybacks so the trailers face the correct direction for unloading. In steam days loops sometimes were provided to turn locomotives.

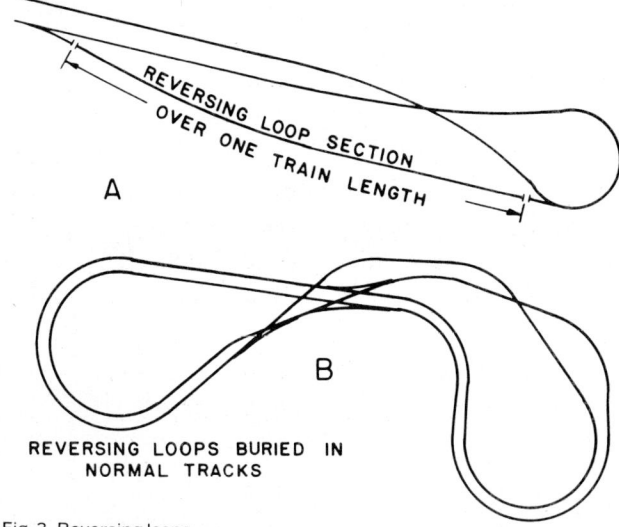

Fig. 3 Reversing loops

On model railroads operated by the two-rail system, AC or DC, reversing loops (and their close relative wyes) require special wiring both for control purposes and to avoid short circuits. Details of such special wiring covering many different applications may be found in the reference cited in Section 5.1 and in almost any other book on model railroad wiring. From a track-design point of view it is only necessary to know that a reversing loop or wye for two-rail must include a section of track electrically isolated (both rails) from all other parts of the railroad and, if short circuits are to be avoided, this reversing-loop or wye section must be at least as long as the longest train. Fig. 3A shows an example where an adequate length of track has been designed into the layout for use as a reversing-loop section. On the other hand reversing loops can be buried in complex trackage so that it is impossible to assign permanently an adequate length of track to serve as a reversing loop section without tying up other routes unnecessarily. An example taken from a published track plan is given at B in Fig. 3. Situations such as Fig. 3B can be handled by providing contacts on the switch machine which convert the necessary track from normal connections to a reversing-loop or wye section as required. Since the electrical problems can be solved through more complex wiring, reversing loops and wyes can be included wherever they are operationally desirable. In many cases a minor change in the track plan will provide the necessary length to a reversing-loop or wye section to bring wiring complexity to its irreducable minimum.

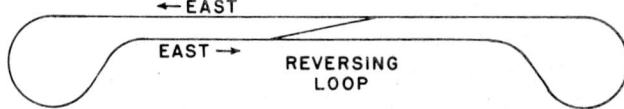

Fig. 4 Double-track illusion

Reversing loops are sometimes unexpectedly added to a two-rail layout in the form of crossovers between apparent double track as shown in the dog-bone layout of Fig. 4. Such crossovers are in fact reversing loops and must be wired as such including the adequate length of reversing-loop section. Particularly if the apparent double track is long and winds out of sight it is easy to forget it is, electrically, two single-track lines running in opposite directions. Even experienced modelers can be fooled as a major club spent some time trying to determine why locomotives would not cross over before they recognized they had a reversing loop.

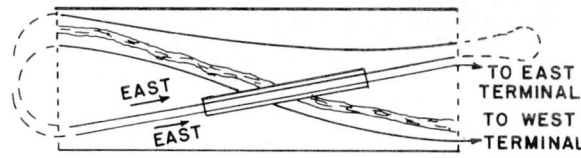

Fig. 5 Simulated double track

When, for scenic reasons, two single-track lines are to be run with the appearance of double track but crossovers are desired between them, if possible select two tracks of the same direction. Fig. 5, a portion of a proposed (1972) N gauge club layout, is an example. Basically this layout was a point-to-point line twice around benchwork projected to be 180' (55m) long but only 2' (.6m) wide. Combining two of the lines into apparent double track opened up the scenery and also made it easier to give the appearance of three different railroads running through the same mountains. Since the direction is the same on both tracks, true crossovers may be installed which would permit a variety of operational concepts.

See Fig. 18, Chapter 7 for types of reversing loops and wyes.

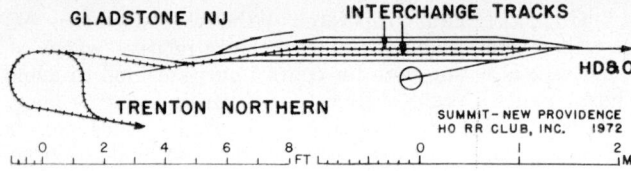

Fig. 6 Interchange tracks

5.4 INTERCHANGE TRACKS

When space permits, interesting operating possibilities are added if the concept includes two independently-operated railroads interchanging freight, possibly even passenger cars or trains. In such cases control of the interchange tracks must be available to either railroad. An example is Gladstone, N.J., DL&W as built in 1949 by the Summit-New Providence HO RR Club, NJ. In 1954 the traction line indicated in Fig. 6 was built and connected to the end of one of the existing tracks at the passenger station. Traction passenger cars did not enter the railroad station tracks but used the reversing loop. Freight motors, on the other hand, had to enter the Gladstone yard to reach the interchange track. Therefore traction cabs had to appear on the railroad cab-control system at the Gladstone tower. This caused operating difficulties for the traction line.

Profiting from the above-mentioned experience, The Model RR Club, which has several interchange points in its plans, has arranged all interchange tracks to be independently accessible by either road so the control of such tracks can be taken over completely by either without disturbing the operation of the other. Fig. 13 Chapter 4, shows the interchange tracks between the traction line and the main line at Jim Thorpe at that club.

As in the case of reversing loops, electrical problems at interchanges can be solved by appropriate circuits so the track design should not be compromised for electrical simplicity but, in most cases, interchange tracks which need only simple controls probably will be equally as satisfactory as those requiring complex controls if electrical considerations are included at the beginning of planning.

Fig. 7 Interlocking signals

5.5 WAYSIDE SIGNALS

Wayside signals add scenic interest even if non-working and such signals need be placed considering only prototype practice, see the reference cited in Section 5.1 for such information. However working signals are even more effective as scenery and, if properly designed, assist operation. Signal circuits can be designed for any track pattern. But if prototype practice is kept in mind, it may be possible to design the track to simplify the signal circuits. Fig. 7 shows how moving a branch junction away from a crossing simplifies one form of non-sticking interlocking signals at the crossing.

5.6 DESIGN FOR SECTIONALIZATION

It is outside the scope of this Handbook to cover the requirements for dividing the layout into sections for independent control of locomotives, see the reference cited in Section 5.1. Nevertheless layout design has much to do with the simplicity of circuits and the ease of control.

In most cases a detailed examination of sectionalization can be deferred until final design (Chapter 9). At that time it will often be found that a minor revision in the track will permit a more logical division of sections.

Note in this Handbook the word 'section' is distinguished from 'block' in accordance with prototype practice. Unfortunately starting about 1941 some model railroaders commenced using the word 'block' ambiguously for either 'block' or 'section.' The prototype definition of 'block' as given by the 1974 Penn Central Rule Book is, "A length of track of defined limits, the use of which by trains and engines is governed by block signals, block-limit signals, cab signals, or cab signals and block signals." In contract 'sections' are used to supply power as shown by the Electrical Operating Instructions of the same railroad, "The third rail is divided into sections and the power supply is controlled by circuit breakers and sectionalization switches."

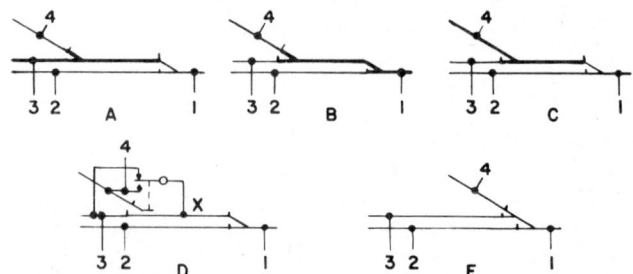

Fig. 8 Section connections

For the minimum complexity of wiring and the greatest ease of operation, sections should be as long as possible without unduly limiting operational flexibility. Locations in which an extra short section appears to be required should be examined to see if a redesign of the track might eliminate that section without operational or scenic penalty. An example is given in Fig. 8 where a long spur with independent control diverges from a siding. For operation it is acceptable that a long train on the siding can block the entrance to the spur. However if the turnout to the spur and the end of the siding is made part of any of the three adjacent sections 1, 3, or 4, restrictions are placed on operation. At A section 3 is required for any move from 1 to 4, at B section 1 is required to move a long train from 3 into the siding. At C section 4 is required for a move involving only the siding. At D a new short section has been created which in effect extends either 3 or 4 automatically depending on the setting of the switch. Sections such as this which receive their power automatically depending on route are often called X sections and provide operating flexibility at the expense of wiring (Section 5.7). However all problems are solved merely by moving the spur switch to the end of the siding as at E.

5.7 X SECTIONS

X Sections, also called by other names, are sections which receive power from an adjacent section depending on the route set by the track switches. In effect an X Section

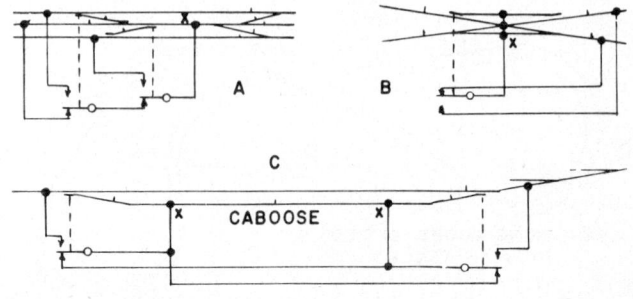

Fig. 9 X Sections

is an automatic extension of that adjacent section and is one of the great simplifiers of wiring and control complexity. To a layout designer the important point is to arrange the track so it is easy and logical to wire for X Sections.

A major use for X Sections is for short sections which form a part of two or more routes such as that shown at A in Fig. 9, also the section marked X in Fig. 8D. The important design point is to make such sections short so they will be cleared quickly by locomotives passing over them. Slip switches as at B often are best arranged as X Sections.

A different type of X Section is shown by the caboose track at C. If only one track switch is thrown to the caboose track, the entire track is controlled from the approaching section at that end. If both switches are thrown to the caboose track, that track is divided so it can be worked by two locomotives simultaneously, one from each end. The layout designer is concerned only with locating the track switches so they logically are in two different sections.

5.8 CONTROL PANELS

The number and type of control panels are functions of the size of the layout and its method of control. The construction and wiring of panels is covered in the reference cited in Section 5.1 but their location and physical type such as vertical, horizontal etc. is an important part of layout design.

Fig. 9 shows several of the types of panels which have been used. The fixed vertical panel at A saves space but is difficult to see from a normal operating position. It has found its greatest application on portable layouts and for panels which are not actively used. Slanted panels as at B are the most popular as they can be conveniently operated either sitting or standing. For the same layout area, a horizontal panel, C, provides the least panel space but may be the best choice in front of low scenery.

Combined slanting and vertical panels, as at D or panels at two different angles suit special conditions. On the layout shown in Fig. 21, Chapter 7 the engineer cab panels were slanted and a vertical Belvidere tower panel mounted above the cabs. For high benchwork a recessed panel, E, saves space but creates access problems to the underside of any track over the panel.

Panels may be elevated and surrounded by a building as shown in Fig. 9 F. This method adds large buildings to the scenery, buildings of the type for which there is seldom room to provide as scenery items. The freight house shown in Fig. 7, Chapter 7 is built around a panel in this fashion.

In confined spaces, panels can be built as drawers to retract under the benchwork as at G or to swing up into operating position as at H. Such construction is not convenient and must be justified by compelling design reasons.

Bruce Chubb and others in the Grand Rapids, Mich. area have found overhead panels such as at I not only space savers but also feel such panels are easier to operate than the conventional low panels. The hump yard of Fig. 9 Chapter 11 is designed for such a panel.

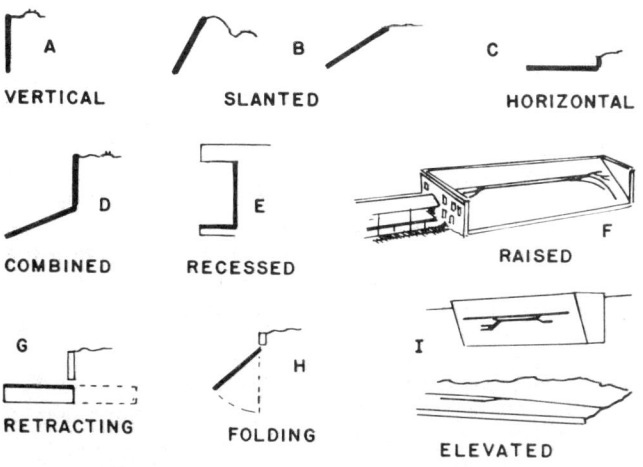

Fig. 10 Panels

Fig. 11. The Model Railroad Club's Rahway River RR panel is neat and compact. At left are special buttons used to activate show loop, used during public viewings when spectators are more interested in seeing trains run aimlessly rather than in a prototypical manner which the general public would not understand.

CHAPTER 6
TRACKWORK

6.1 GENERAL

This chapter covers design for tracks but not their construction. The latter information may be found in the Trackwork Handbook for Model Railroads by the same author and published by the Boynton & Associates. Special information of street-car and interurban track is included in the Model Traction Handbook, also by the same author but published by Vane Jones, 6710 Hampton Dr. E., Indianapolis, IN 46226.

Trackwork standards should be adopted before preliminary design starts. Such standards assure reliable operation over all parts of the layout and should, initially, be set as high as seems practical. If standards prove too stringent, they can and will be relaxed. On the other hand it is difficult to improve standards at a later date particularly if it means eliminating tracks which could be included with lower standards.

Some design standards can be expressed as numbers, for example, minimum radius and maximum distance from an access aisle. Other standards are statements such as, 'No curved turnouts', and, 'No turnouts in tunnels'. If switching with automatic couplers is part of the concept, tracks on which coupling regularly takes place should have standards for minimum radius based on the operating capabilities of the selected coupler. (Section 6.8).

Once standards are adopted which are reasonable for the space available and the type of railroad, they should be followed without exception. Substandard track put in here and there for the sake of gaining an extra track may well introduce problems.

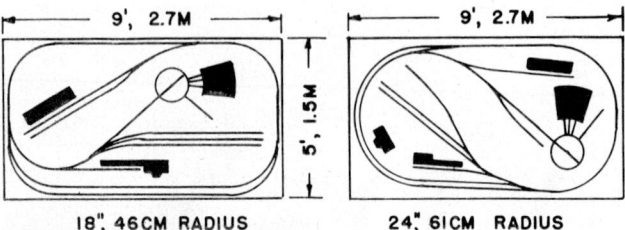

Fig. 1 Maximizing radii

6.2 CURVES

Minimum radius

No standard is more important to layout design or to reliable operation than the minimum radius adopted. On a small layout the space available often sets an upper bound to the minimum radii which can be considered. The soundest rule is to adopt the widest practical radius as the minimum. As an illustration, the two HO layouts of Fig. 1 are for the same 5' by 9' (1.5 by 2.7m) table benchwork and both have a single main-line station concept. The one on the left uses 18" (46cm) radius, the one on the right 24" (61cm). Obviously the one on the left can have more tracks and handle somewhat longer trains but it will be necessary to be quite selective of the cars and motive power to be able to operate over such radii. The layout on the right is less restrictive of equipment, will operate better, and has a better appearance.

Even when space permits very large radii, for many benchwork types, access considerations often limit the minimum radius to 4' (1.2m) or less regardless of scale (Section 3.2). An important advantage of either around-the-room shelf or rabbit-warren benchwork is the very large minimum radii which can be adopted yet retaining excellent access.

Often it is desirable to set more than one minimum radius, for example 4' (1.2m) on the main, 3'6" (1.1m) on a branch, and 3' (.9) in yards. Such minimums will operate well with almost all HO equipment. Specifically, if automatic coupling is to be used, a minimum radius should be set for tracks on which coupling normally takes place (Section 6.8).

If space does not permit large radii, it is important to select locomotives and equipment which will operate reliably on the curves which are to be built. When space is particularly limited, consideration should be given to prototypes which justify tight radii such as interurbans, street cars, and narrow gauge, or to a concept which does not require loops, for example a switching line. One of these choices might be far superior to forcing a standard railroad into a small area.

Fig. 2 is a table of radii for N, HO and O scales, their relationship to the prototype, and the type of standard gauge service for which they are suitable. This table assumes normal model railroad equipment with body-mounted couplers.

Do not forget the overhang of cars and locomotives on curves. See Section 6.9 for the increased clearance required on short-radii curves.

MODEL RADIUS			PROTOTYPE		MINIMUM FOR USE
N	HO	O	Radius	Degree	
2.62" 6.7cm	4.8" 12.2cm	8.75" 10.7cm	35' 10.7m	-	Sharp radius street car, model and prototype
3.8" 9.7cm	7" 17.8cm	12.7" 32.3cm	50.8' 15.5m	-	Conventional street car models
5.44" 13.8cm	10" 25.4cm	18.1" 46cm	72.5' 22.1m	-	Heavy street cars, small interurban models
7.5" 19cm	13.8" 35cm	25" 63cm	100' 30.5m	60	Common prototype int. radius, industrial,
9.8" 24.9cm	18" 45.7cm	32.6" 83cm	130.6' 39.8m	45	Short cars, locos on model Very tight proto. yard
13" 33cm	24" 61cm	43.5" 1.1m	174.2' 53.1m	32.9	All but longest cars, locos on model. Short proto. yd.
22.9" 58cm	42" 1.07m	76.2" 1.94m	304.9' 92.9m	18.9	Any model equipment
26.9" 68cm	49.5" 1.26m	89.8" 2.28m	359.3' 109.5m	16	Tight radius for heavy steam locos
39.2" 99cm	72" 1.83m	131" 3.3m	522' 159m	11	Sharp prototype mainline curve.

Fig. 2 Minimum standard gauge radii

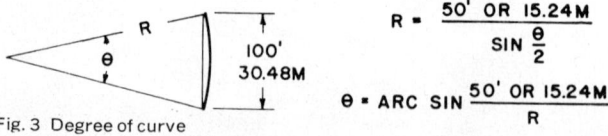

Fig. 3 Degree of curve

Degree of Curve

In U.S. and Canadian prototype practice the sharpness of a curve is measured in degrees in contrast to model and European prototype practice where radius is the measure. The degree of a curve is the central angle, in Fig. 3, which is subtended by a 100' (30.48m) chord. Knowing either the radius or the degree, the other can be calculated by the formulas given in the figure. The table of Fig. 4 gives the prototype and the N, HO, and O gauge radii corresponding to degrees. This table differs somewhat from published tables which use the simplifying approximation of dividing the radius of a 1° curve by the number of degrees.

Degree	PROTOTYPE Feet	PROTOTYPE meters	RADIUS N Ft. & In.	RADIUS N cm	RADIUS HO Ft. & In.	RADIUS HO CM	RADIUS O Ft. & In.	RADIUS O CM
1	5730	1746	35'10"	1091	65'9"	2005	119'5"	3638
2	2865	873	17'11"	546	32'11"	1002	59'8"	1819
3	1910	582	11'11"	363.8	21'11"	668	39'10"	1213
4	1433	437	8'11"	273.1	16'5"	502	29'10"	910
5	1146	349	7'2"	218.1	13'2"	401	23'11"	727
6	955	291	5'11.6"	181.9	11'0"	334.1	19'11"	606
7	819	250	5'1.4"	156.3	9'5"	287.0	17'1"	521
8	717	218	4'5.8"	136.3	8'3"	250.3	14'11"	454
9	637	194	3'11.8"	121.3	7'4"	222.7	13'3"	404
10	574	175	3'7.1"	109.4	6'7"	200.9	11'11"	365
11	522	159	3'3.2"	99.4	6'0"	182.5	10'11"	331.3
12	478	145.8	2'11.9"	91.1	5'5.9"	167.4"	10'0"	303.8
13	442	134.6	2'9.2"	84.1	5'0.9"	154.5	9'2"	280.4
14	410	125.1	2'6.8"	78.2	4'8.5"	143.6	8'7"	260.6
15	383	116.8	2'4.7"	73.0	4'4.8"	134.1	8'0"	243.3
16	359.3	109.5	2'2.9"	68.4	4'1.5"	125.7	7'5.8"	228.1
17	338.3	103.1	2'1.4"	64.4	3'10.6"	118.4	7'0.6"	214.8
18	319.6	97.4	2'0"	60.9	3'7.9"	111.1	6'7.8"	202.9
19	302.9	92.3	1'10.7"	57.7	3'5.7"	106.0	6'3.7"	192.3
20	287.9	87.8	1'9.6"	54.9	3'3.7"	100.8	6'0.0"	182.9
21	274.4	83.6	1'8.6"	52.3	3'1.8"	96.0	5'8.6"	174.2
22	262.0	79.9	1'7.7"	49.9	3'0.1"	91.7	5'5.5"	166.5
23	250.8	76.4	1'6.8"	47.8	2'10.6"	87.7	5'2.7"	159.2
24	240.5	73.3	1'6.0"	45.8	2'9.1"	84.2	5'0.1"	152.7
25	231.0	70.4	1'5.3"	44.0	2'7.8"	80.8	4'9.8"	146.7
26	222.3	67.7	1'4.7"	42.3	2'6.6"	77.7	4'7.6"	141.0
27	214.3	65.3	1'4.1"	40.8	2'5.5"	75.0	4'5.6"	136.0
28	206.7	63.0	1'3.5	39.4	2'4.5"	72.3	4'3.7"	131.3
29	199.7	60.9	1'3"	38.1	2'3.5"	69.9	4'1.9"	126.9
30	193.2	58.9	1'2.5"	36.8	2'2.6"	67.6	4'0.3"	122.7
32	181.4	55.3	1'1.6"	34.6	2'1.0	63.5	3'9.4"	115.2
34	171.0	52.1	1'0.8"	32.6	1'11.6"	59.8	3'6.8"	108.5
36	161.8	49.3	1'0.1"	30.8	1'10.3"	56.6	3'4.4"	102.7
38	153.6	46.8	11.5"	29.3	1'9.2"	53.8	3'2.4"	97.7
40	146.2	44.6	11.0"	27.9	1'8.1"	51.2	3'0.5"	92.9
42	139.5	42.5	10.5"	26.6	1'7.2"	48.8	2'10.9"	88.5
44	133.5	40.7	10.1"	25.4	1'6.4"	46.7	2'9.4"	84.8
46	128.0	39.0	9.6"	24.4	1'5.6"	44.8	2'8.0"	81.3
48	122.9	37.5	9.2"	23.4	1'4.9"	43.1	2'6.7"	78.1
50	118.3	36.1	8.9"	22.6	1'4.3"	41.4	2'5.6"	75.2
52	114.1	34.8	8.6"	21.8	1'3.7"	40.0	2'4.5"	72.5
54	110.1	33.6	8.3"	21.0	1'3.2"	38.6	2'3.5"	70.0
56	106.5	32.5	8.0"	20.3	1'2.7"	37.3	2'2.6"	67.7
58	103.1	31.4	7.7"	19.6	1'2.2"	36.1	2'1.8"	65.4
60	100.0	30.5	7.5"	19.1	1'1.8"	35.0	2'1.0"	63.5
65	93.1	28.4	7.0"	17.8	1'0.8"	32.6	1'11.3"	59.2
70	87.2	26.6	6.5"	16.6	1'0.0"	30.5	1'9.8"	55.4
75	82.1	25.0	6.2"	15.6	11.3"	28.7	1'8.5"	52.1
80	77.8	23.7	5.8"	14.8	10.7"	27.2	1'7.4"	49.4
85	74.0	22.6	5.6"	14.1	10.2"	25.9	1'6.5"	47.1
90	70.7	21.6	5.3"	13.5	9.7"	24.8	1'5.7"	45.0
100	65.3	19.9	4.9"	12.4	9.0"	22.8	1'4.3"	41.5
125	56.4	17.2	4.2"	10.8	7.8"	19.7"	1'2.1"	35.8
150	51.8	15.8	3.9"	9.9	7.1"	18.1	1'1.0"	32.9
180	50	15.2	3.8"	9.5	6.9"	17.5	1'0.5"	31.7

Fig. 4 Degrees corresponding to radii

Easements

At the point where a tangent (straight) track is connected directly to a circular (constant-radius) curve as on the left in Fig. 5, there is a sudden change in direction. The lurch of trains at that point looks bad even on large-radius curves, also there is a tendency for the flanges to climb over the outside rail of the curve. Leading a tangent directly into a short-radius curve may cause the swing of the couplers in their pockets to be exceeded with consequent derailments (Section 6.8). Similar problems, but of lesser impact, occur when two circular curves of different radii are connected together.

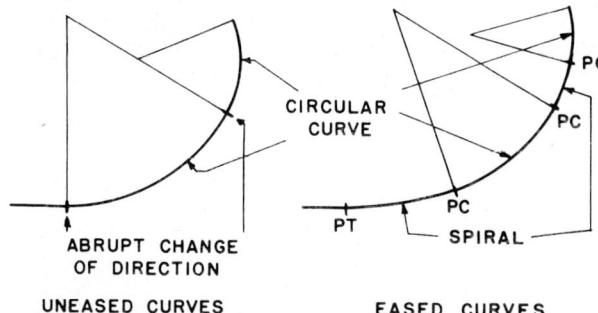

Fig. 5 Easement spirals

Appearance will be improved and the possibility of derailments reduced if the prototype practice of connecting a tangent to a circular curve by a spiral (also known as an easement or a transition curve) is followed as on the right in Fig. 5. In addition to making a smooth connection to a circular curve or between two circular curves, on the prototype the easement also allows for superelevation run off, that is the dropping of the elevated outer rail (banked track) on a curve to the same level as the other rail when the tangent is reached.

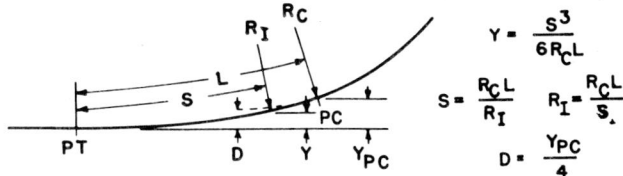

Fig. 6 Cubic spiral

$$Y = \frac{S^3}{6R_C L}$$

$$S = \frac{R_C L}{R_I} \quad R_I = \frac{R_C L}{S}$$

$$D = \frac{Y_{PC}}{4}$$

Any form of a spiral which changes smoothly from a tangent to a given radius can be used for an easement but perhaps the most popular for this purpose is the cubic spiral shown in Fig. 6. PT (point of tangency) is the point where the spiral starts to curve away from the tangent. PC (point of curvature) is the point where the spiral reaches the radius of the circular curve, RC. L is the length along the spiral from PT to PC. For any given distance S along the spiral, the spiral is displaced a distance Y from the tangent extension. For any given S there is an intermediate radius RI. When S = L, RI = RC and Y = YPC. D is the displacement of the extension of the circular curve from the extension of the tangent. All dimensions are in the same units. In the examples given, inches are used but they could have been cm as well.

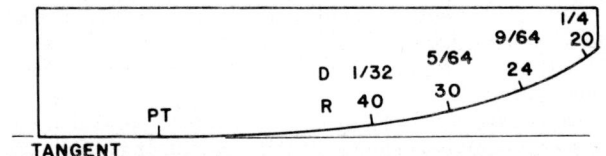

Fig. 7 Easement template

The equations of Fig. 6 can be used to calculate any desired spiral. Note that spirals have nothing to do with scale or gauge, a 12" spiral leading to a 24" radius is exactly the same for N, HO, or O. Any length spiral may be used for any radius curve but, as a practical matter on a model, a length approximately one-third to one-fourth the circular-curve radius is a good compromise.

Once a spiral has been calculated, those dimensions can be used to lay out a template such as the one shown in Fig. 7. Since the spiral will match any radius down to the shortest calculated, intermediate radii together with their associated offsets 'D' can be marked as indicated. The centerline of the curve is drawn offset from the tangent by the distance D and the template slid along the tangent until it matches the curve.

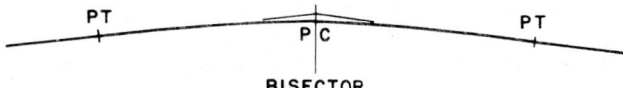

Fig. 8 Easements back to back

When only a slight bend is to be made in main tracks, it is effective and convenient to use two easements which meet at the bisector of the tangent extensions as shown in Fig. 8. A spiral is also the best way of joining two circular curves. However, the use of templates to lay out track is outside the scope of this Handbook. A complete description of such techniques as well as tables for spirals plus one printed easement template may be found in the reference cited in Section 6.1.

Chapter 6

25

It is impractical to show easements on plans drawn to the usual scales, even as large as 1½" = 1' (8:1). The offset distance D will be lost in the line widths on the drawing. Plans are drawn with the circular curve leading directly into the tangent. The easement is added when the track is laid out full size on the roadbed. Remember that the spiral projects approximately one-half its length along the tangent line on the plans.

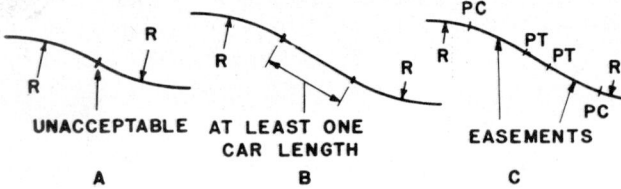

Fig. 9 Reverse curves

Reverse Curves

When a curve leads directly into another curve of opposite direction as indicated at A in Fig. 9, the combination is called a reverse curve. Butting two short-radii circular curves together in this manner is virtually certain to cause derailments not only because of the sudden change in direction but also because the couplers may not be able to swing far enough in their pockets (Section 6.8). Reverse curves of the type shown at A *must* be avoided, there can be no exceptions to this rule. As a minimum there *must* be a length of tangent between the curves at B. This tangent should be as long as the longest car to allow every car to straighten out before it starts swinging the other way. A half-car length of tangent will give passable operation provided the curves are not so short as to exceed coupler swing.

The best solution for reverse curves is a pair of easements as indicated at C. There should be some tangent between the two PT's but, if the easements are long, its length is not critical.

A conventional crossover between two parallel tracks is a reverse curve as shown at A in Fig. 10. It is important that the frogs of turnouts used for crossovers be straight to maximize the length of tangent between the two curves. Most model equipment will pass a No. 6 crossover but it is quite possible that equipment which will take a No. 4 turnout which does not lead into a reverse curve will not negotiate a No. 4 crossover even if the frogs are straight.

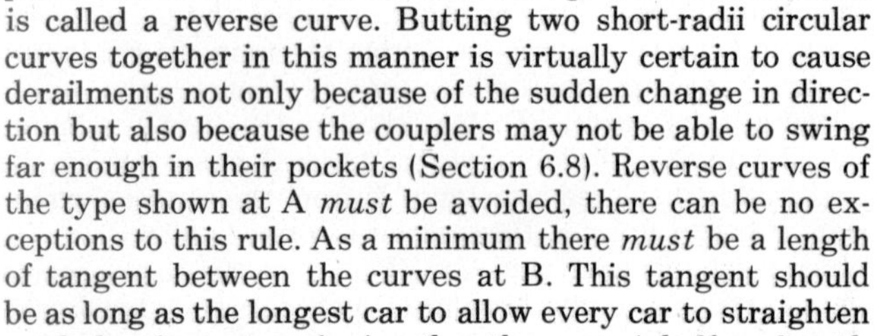

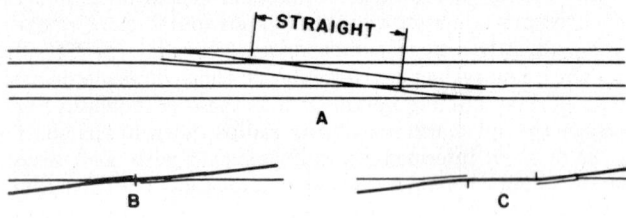

Fig. 10 Turnout reverse curves

Turnouts point-to-point as in Fig. 10B also create a reverse curve for the route shown by the heavy line. Either the points should be very close together so the two turnouts essentially become a movable-point crossing (Fig. 25) for the heavy-line route at B in Fig. 10 or there should be one car-length between the points as at C.

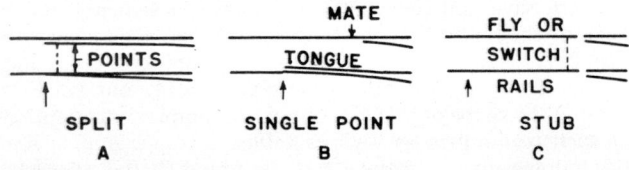

Fig. 11 Switches

6.3 TURNOUTS AND SPECIAL SWITCHES

Switch

A switch is a device for changing a wheel from one rail to another. The split switch, A in Fig. 11, is the most common. Tracks in the street often use tongue switches, also called single-point switches if there is a tongue switch in only one rail as at B. Stub switches, C, were common before World War I and were still in use on the White Pass and Yukon in 1970. For layout design only the locations of the points as indicated by the arrows in Fig. 11 are of importance.

Switches require maintenance and also present the single greatest derailment hazard on a model railroad. They should always be in readily-accessible locations. If they must be in a tunnel, it is essential that the scenery over the tunnel be removable. An expedient to justify scenically a switch in a single-track line leading directly into a double-track tunnel (so placed to keep the switch in the open) is a model of an abandoned second track alongside the exposed single-track line (Fig. 7, Chapter 7).

If the train approaches the switches of Fig. 11 from the left, the switch controls the route of the train and is said to be **facing**. If a train approaches from the right, there is no choice of route and the switch is called **trailing**. Unless a switch is used to control the routing of trains, an effort should be made to design for a trailing switch on any track which has a predominate direction of traffic. Trailing switches present a lesser derailment hazard.

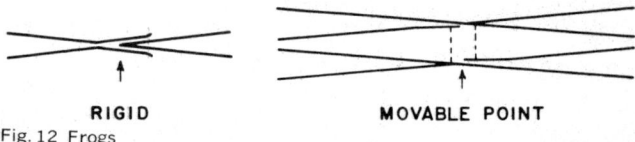

Fig. 12 Frogs

Frog

A frog is a device for allowing a wheel to cross another rail. Two types are of importance on a model, rigid as on the left in Fig. 12 and movable point as on the right. Although the points of a movable-point frog are similar to those of a split switch, their purpose is just the opposite for the points of a frog prevent a wheel from changing from one rail to another. Movable-point frogs are required for the center (obtuse) frogs of crossings of 10° or less and those of slip switches No. 8 or larger to guarantee wheels will not diverge to the wrong route. For layout design only the point of the crossing rails, indicated by the arrows in Fig. 12, is of importance.

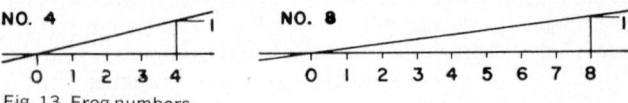

Fig. 13 Frog numbers

Small-angle frogs, such as the rigid frog shown in Fig. 12, are designated by the number of units along one rail to the point where the other rail has diverged one unit (in mathematics the cotangent). In other words a No. 4 frog diverges one unit for every four units as indicated on the left in Fig. 13 and a No. 8 diverges one unit for every eight units as shown on the right.

Large-angle frogs are designated by the degrees between the crossing rails, e.g., a 45° frog. The angles in degrees corresponding to frog numbers are given in the table of Fig. 14.

Frogs on prototype railroads are almost always straight, that is the crossing rails are straight for a distance on both sides of the point of the frog. For realistic appearance and for greatest reliability, model frogs should be straight. This particularly applies to the frogs of crossovers (Fig. 10) and of crossings. Street cars, however, often used curved frogs to save space. When a curved frog can be guarded, they work well as the guard rail will keep the flange from striking the point of the frog.

The proper construction and the electrical connections for frogs and switches are vital but outside the scope of this Handbook. Such information is available in the references cited in Sections 5.1 and 6.1.

Frog No.	Degrees	Frog. No.	Degrees
3	18.4	12	4.8
4	14.0	13	4.4
5	11.3	14	4.1
6	9.5	15	3.8
7	8.1	16	3.6
8	7.1	17	3.4
9	6.3	18	3.2
10	5.7	19	3.0
11	5.2	20	2.9

Fig. 14 Frog angles

Turnouts

A turnout is the assembly of a switch, a frog, and associated rails to permit one track to turn out from another track. In its most common form one track is straight and the other curved as shown on the left in Fig. 15. When the tracks curve in opposite directions as at the center, it is called a wye turnout or a wye switch. When both wye tracks curve equally, particularly on a wide radius for high speed service it may be called an equilateral turnout. The straight and wye turnouts are equally reliable.

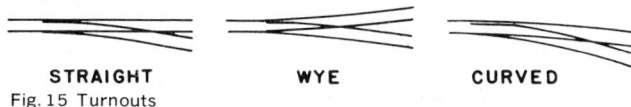

STRAIGHT   WYE   CURVED

Fig. 15 Turnouts

When both tracks curve in the same direction it is called a curved turnout as on the right in Fig. 15. Because the flanges tend to press against the outside rail on a curve the chance of a derailment at a curved turnout is distinctly greater than at a straight or wye turnout particularly if the track approaching the points is also curved. Curved turnouts should not be designed into a layout unless there is some significant advantage. For the same reason the rails approaching the points of any switch should be straight, preferably for one car length.

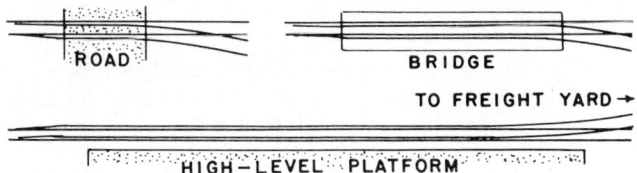

ROAD   BRIDGE
              TO FREIGHT YARD →
              HIGH-LEVEL PLATFORM

Fig. 16 Gantlet turnouts

Fig. 16 shows gantlet (also spelled gauntlet) turnouts in which the switch and the frog are separated by gantlet track (Section 6.5). Gantlet turnouts are used on the prototype when the points would otherwise be in an unsatisfactory position as in the middle of a highway grade crossing as at the upper left in the figure. Rapid City, S.D. had such an installation in 1974. They are also used to keep the switch off the bridge, the Rutland having had such an example at Bellows Falls, Vt. This application is particularly suited to model railroads when switch machines are mounted under the track. The South Shore had a gantlet turnout as at the bottom of the figure to move freight cars away from the high passenger platforms at Gary, Indiana.

Turnouts are known by the number of their frog, e.g., a No. 8 turnout has a No. 8 frog. This only defines a straight turnout for the number of the frog on a wye or curved turnout will depend on the curvature of the tracks. For the same number frog a wye turnout will be more gentle and a curved turnout more abrupt than a straight turnout. The minimum frog number for straight turnouts is an important standard to set before starting design work.

When a series of turnouts, possibly also slip switches, provides access to parallel tracks the combination is called a ladder (Section 7.7).

As far as model operation is concerned, a No. 4 turnout not leading into a reverse curve such as in a crossover will handle equipment which can take a 2′ (.6m) radius in HO (11″, 33 cm in N; 3′7″, 109cm in O) and a No. 6 all but long locomotives and cars and even such equipment can be built to take a No. 6. Appearance is something else. A passenger train taking a No. 6 crossover does not look realistic. No. 8 is about the minimum found on the prototype to handle mainline equipment and, except for the smallest of layouts, can be fitted into model plans. No. 10 crossovers often are used on main tracks by the prototype and present an excellent appearance on the model. There seems little reason for going larger than No. 10 as the points begin to get long and consequently weak. There are modelers who feel turnouts should be kept short to create a greater illusion of distance along the track. This argument must be balanced against the impression caused by the unrealistic violent motion between car ends as well as fidelity to prototype.

If there are various types of track, in most cases it is best to adopt a specific minimum turnout number for each distinct type. As a practical example, The Model Railroad Club after 22 years of experience on its first layout which had a No. 8 minimum turnout on all its standard-gauge railroad tracks, yard as well as main line, adopted the following standards in 1970 for its new railroad: Main line, No. 10; Branch and yard, No. 8; Industrial switching track, No. 6. If space is critical, turnouts which do not lead into a reverse curve can be one number smaller than those of crossovers and sidings. See 'Reverse Curves' in Section 6.2.

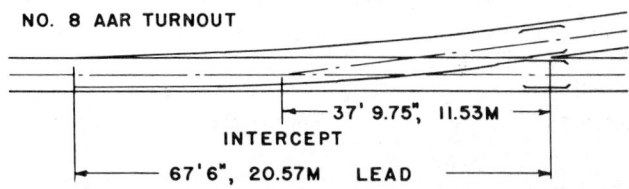

NO. 8 AAR TURNOUT

|← 37′ 9.75″, 11.53M →|
INTERCEPT
|← 67′6″, 20.57M LEAD →|

Fig. 17 Complete turnout

Fig. 17 shows a complete turnout and indicates the position of the switch points, the point of the frog, the distance between the switch points and the frog (the lead), and the distance from the frog to the intercept of the centerlines of the two tracks. It is these two distances plus the angle of the frog which are of importance to layout design. The table of Fig. 18 lists these important dimensions based on AAR (Association of American Railroads) standard turnouts both full size for the prototype and for N, HO, and O gauges. Other prototype turnout tables exist for turnouts with straight switch point rails but they differ only slightly from the AAR tables. Prototype turnouts have been built with curved points but seldom for railroad. Tables for such turnouts may be found in RP12 of the NMRA.

		Frog Number							
		4		6		8		10	
Lead	Prototype	37′	11.28m	48.4′	14.75m	67.5′	20.6m	77.5′	23.2m
	N	2.8″	70mm	3.6″	92mm	5″	129mm	5.8″	148mm
	HO	5.1″	130mm	6.7″	169mm	9.3″	236mm	10.7″	271mm
	O	9.2″	235mm	12.1″	307mm	16.9″	429mm	19.4″	492mm
Intercept	Prototype	19.1′	5.8m	28.5′	8.7m	37.8′	11.5m	47.2′	11.4m
	N	1.4″	36mm	2.1″	53mm	2.8″	72mm	3.5″	90mm
	HO	2.6″	67mm	3.9″	100mm	5.2″	132mm	6.5″	165mm
	O	4.8″	122mm	7.1″	180mm	9.5″	240mm	11.8″	300mm

Fig. 18 Turnout dimensions

Although the dimensions of Fig. 18 are sufficient for layout design, more are needed to construct a turnout and the necessary information may be found in the reference given in Section 6.1 as well as in almost every other comprehensive model railroad manual or prototype engineering book. In prototype tables both a 'practical' and a 'theoretical' lead will be found. The theoretical lead is measured to the actual crossing of the gauge lines (as indicated in Fig. 17 and called lead). However prototype frogs have blunted points and the practical lead is measured from the blunted point rather than the gauge-line crossing.

Some of the commercial turnouts, especially of the prefabricated type, have not followed prototype dimensions closely. In at least one case a turnout marketed as a No. 8 actually had a frog just slightly greater than a No. 7. If commercial turnouts are to be installed, base the design on the dimensions taken from those particular units.

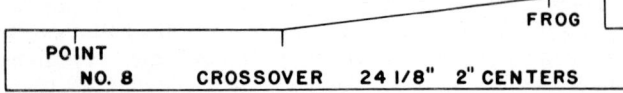

Fig. 19 Turnout template

Even on preliminary plans it is important to indicate accurately the location of the switch points, the frog, the intercept, and the centerline of the diverging track. Experience has shown that modelers tend to underestimate the distance required to install a turnout and to indicate too sharp a frog angle when drawing plans. To avoid such problems and to speed the work it is helpful to cut simple templates similar to that shown in Fig. 19. The templates are, of course, made to the scale of the drawings. Similar templates made full size for the particular gauge will be useful in transfering the plans onto the roadbed. Because crossovers are frequent, it is helpful to note on the template the length between points of a crossover using that turnout on tangent track at normal spacings. In Fig. 19 2" centers for HO tracks are assumed. In laying out a crossover on a drawing, mark the points in using a scale to get the correct distance then place the template to draw in the crossover track.

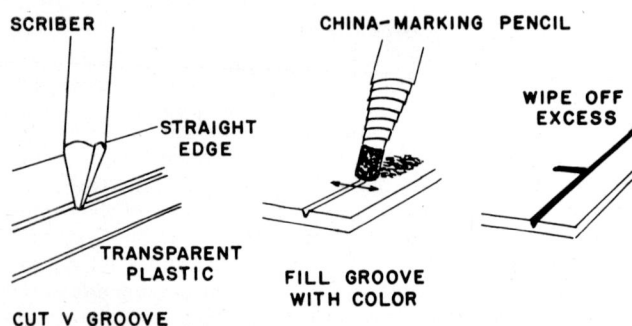

Fig. 20 Making transparent templates

Templates can be cut from card stock but transparent material such as acetate is better as lines already drawn on the plans can be seen through such templates. The lines on the template are scribed with a V-shaped tool filed from a nail as shown in Fig. 20. The V grooves are then filled with colored wax by rubbing them with a china-marking (grease) pencil and the excess cleaned with a cloth. A self-stick label provides a place to write the information and also makes it easier to find the template for, being transparent, it tends to disappear when on a drawing.

Lap Switches

Two turnouts facing in opposite directions can be installed with overlaping leads as indicated in Fig. 21, the combination being called a lap switch. A lap switch could be considered a gantlet crossover. Prototype examples built

Fig. 21 Lap switches

as such were rare, there was one near the Jacksonville, Fla. passenger terminal. Sometimes, however, as traffic decreased, slip switches were converted into lap switches to reduce maintenance. On a model lap switches present no more operating hazards than two straight turnouts and may be useful in tight spaces. The turnout template of Fig. 19 can be used to lay out a lap switch. Be sure there is enough distance between the points of one turnout and the frog of the other that there is no interference. A guard rail ending just before a point improves the reliability of that switch.

Fig. 22 Three-way switches

Three-Way Switches

Two turnouts facing in the same direction can be installed with overlaping leads as indicated in Fig. 22, this type of lap switch being called a three-way switch (other names are sometimes used). When the points close on each other as on the left in Fig. 22, derailment hazard is increased both at the switch and on the center route if the frogs are directly opposite each other. However the tandem type (sometimes called staggered), except for the added frog, is essentially no different than two turnouts in succession. Straight turnout templates can be used to layout either type of three-way switch.

On prototype railroads three-way switches are rare except in hump yards. They were more common when stub switches were in use and in 1972 a stub three-way switch was still in service at the engine terminal of the East Broad Top. Tandem three-way switches were common on streetcar systems.

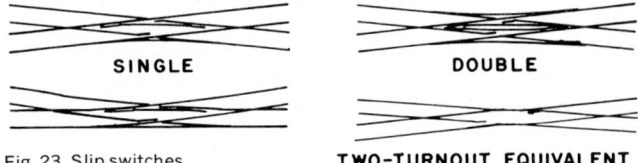

Fig. 23 Slip switches

Slip Switches

Slip switches are a crossing with switches inside the diamond of the crossing to permit a train to transfer from one track to the other. A single slip switch as on the left in Fig. 23 has one such slip route. A double slip switch as on the right has two. In the case of a single slip, the slip route may be straight with the crossing routes curved as at the lower left of the figure. The New Haven had such a slip switch at Springfield, Mass. but this type was rare on the prototype. Slip switches are known by the number of their acute frogs, e.g. a No. 8 double slip.

A double slip switch employs four switches and a crossing for a task which can be accomplished by two turnouts. On both the prototype and model a slip switch greatly increases the maintenance required and, on the model, increases the chance of derailments. North American railroad practice avoids slip switches except in locations where space is expensive such as terminals or in congested areas such as at transfer bridges. Rapid transit lines use them extensively, for example the PATH system between N.Y. and N.J., and they were found to some extent on street car lines. In 1974 one was still in service at the Reservoir car barns in Boston. European practice uses slip switches extensively, even to serve one-car spurs.

In their construction details slip switches are complex but, for the purposes of layout design, they can be drawn as a simple crossing plus an indication of the slip routes as slip switches take no more room than a crossing. However, for No. 6 and sharper slip switches, check for clearance required for overhang (Section 6.9).

Fig. 24 Overlapped switches and crossing

Switches and a crossing can be overlapped with the switch points outside the diamond of the crossing as shown in Fig. 24. Such arrangements are not slip switches although they accomplish the same purpose. They were seldom, if ever, used by railroads but were not uncommon on inter-urban and street-car lines, the Red Arrow had many at its 69th St. terminal in Philadelphia.

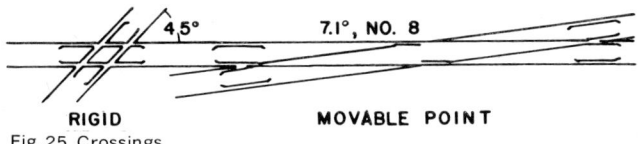

Fig. 25 Crossings

6.4 CROSSINGS

Crossings, also called diamonds due to their shape, have four frogs to permit two tracks to cross at grade. Crossings are designated by the acute angle between the crossing tracks, a 45° crossing and a 7.1° are shown in Fig. 25. When the angle is that normally associated with a numbered frog, the crossing may be called by that number, for example the 7.1° crossing of Fig. 25 probably would be called a No. 8 crossing. Except for a 90° crossing there are two obtuse (center) and two acute (end) frogs in the diamond.

When the crossing angle is greater than 15°, guard rails can prevent wheels from diverging to the incorrect track but at angle less than 15°, the openings in the guard rails at the center frogs become nearly opposite each other and cannot prevent a wheel from taking the wrong path. In such cases movable point frogs should be installed and they become more and more a necessity as the angle becomes smaller. For greatest operating reliability, crossings should be designed into the layout with the largest angle feasible.

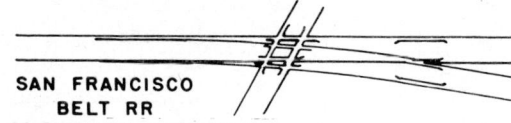

Fig. 26 Crossing through turnout

Large-angle crossings introduce little derailment hazard. They can be readily built with insulated frogs and thus do not add electrical complications on two-rail layouts. Consequently such crossings can be designed into almost any location including between the switch and the frog of a turnout as shown by the prototype example, Fig. 26, which existed in 1972 at Sansome and Chestnut in San Francisco on the San Francisco Belt RR.

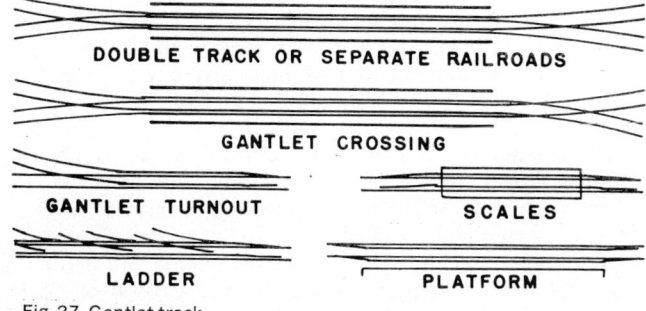

Fig. 27 Gantlet track

6.5 GANTLET TRACK

When two tracks are overlapped as shown in Fig. 27 it is called gantlet (also spelled gauntlet) track. The most common prototype examples of gantlet track are to carry double-track lines over a narrow bridge or through a narrow tunnel without requiring a switch at each end, also for temporary track during construction. There were at least two prototype examples of gantlet track used by two separate lines to cross bridges, one a combination of the Central of Vermont and the Rutland, the other the Boston and Maine and the Concord and Manchester Electric.

If two-rail model gantlet track is for two separate lines, designing the gantlet so that the frogs are in the common rails of both lines eliminates the need for insulated rail gaps or special electrical connections at those frogs.

For all known prototype examples of gantleting two tracks, those tracks separate in the same order at both ends of the gantlet. However there is no reason why the tracks cannot separate in reverse order to form a gantlet crossing. Such a gantlet crossing was installed at the Summit-New Providence HO RR Club. Their traction line and main railroad shared gantlet track over a 5′ (1.5m) trestle in order to reduce the number of bridges at that point as the scenery would otherwise be too cluttered. (Fig 10, Chapter 4).

Gantlet track may be used to extend the lead of a turnout to form the gantlet turnout of Fig. 27, see also Fig. 16. At track scales gantlet track is sometimes provided so locomotives as well as cars not to be weighed need not use the rails on the scale. Switches of a ladder can be placed on a gantlet to get the points off of a service route as at a still-existing (1974) car barn in Philadelphia. The Model Traction Handbook referenced in Section 6.1 has more information on traction usage of gantlets.

Gantlet track existed in 1974 at the Roselle Park, N.J. station of the Lehigh Valley to permit freights with wide cars to move away from the high passenger platform and a gantlet turnout was at Gary, Indiana on the South Shore for the same purpose (Fig. 16). Conversely the main route may be placed away from the platform as at the Capitol Beltway station, Md. with trains making a station stop moving over to the platform on a gantlet. At Manhattan Transfer gantlets were provided on two of the platform tracks so both the narrow Hudson & Manhattan cars and the Pennsylvania RR cars could stop at the same high platforms.

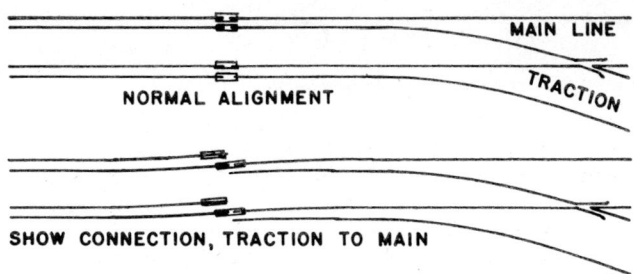

Fig. 28 Temporary routing at gantlet

On a model, gantlet track can be used for all the prototype reasons as well as to create scenic or operational interest. The gantlet track of Fig. 10, Chapter 4, also served for three years an unusual stub lap switch (gantlet crossover) as shown in Fig. 28 for diverting the trains from the railroad to the traction line during the annual public show only.

6.6 GRADES

The maximum grade for a particular line is another important design standard which should be adopted before the start of planning. Grade is expressed in percent, that is the number of units rise for 100 units of run as illustrated in Fig. 29. The table of Fig. 30 is a guide to selecting maxi-

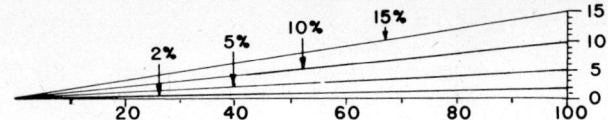

Fig. 29 Percent of grade

mum grades based on grades long enough to contain an entire train. If a grade is short, it could be steeper. Nevertheless most modelers select a maximum and adhere to it for all grades, long or short.

Particularly on small layouts, the maximum grade selected is strongly influenced by the distance available for a track to climb and pass over another track. In metric units the run in meters required for a given rise is the centimeter rise divided by the grade in percent, e.g., to climb 10cm at 2% takes 5m, 10÷2=5. In English units it is close to consider percent as eighths of inch per foot so a 3" rise at 2% requires a run of 12' (3÷2/8=12).

Type of Service		Maximum Grade
Railroad	Main tracks	2%
	Helper grade	3%
	Industrial tracks	5%
	Yard	0.5%
Interurban	Freight	3%
	Passenger only	4%
Streetcar		8%

Fig. 30 A guide to maximum grade

Obvious, but sometimes overlooked, is that dropping one line and raising the other as shown in Fig. 31 halves the distance necessary to gain the same grade separation. See Fig. 11, Chapter 7 for the recommended minimum distances to pass one track over another.

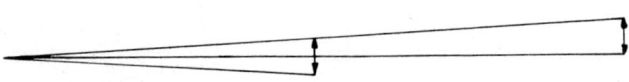

Fig. 31 Minimizing run for grade separation

Even the smallest layout should have two different maximum grades selected. One is the hill-climbing grade, the other for tracks on which cars are left standing. The latter should be set so even the best-rolling car will come to rest if set in motion. ½% is low enough for most cars but ¼% is safer.

Larger layouts with different types of lines might have several different grades selected as maximums. For example in 1969 the following maximum grades were set by The Model Railroad Club for their then-proposed new layout. Railroad: Main line, 1.5% except helper district, 2.5%; Branch line 2%; Yard, .25%; Industrial tracks, 4.5%. Interurban: Interchange freight; 4%; Traction only, 6%.

The maximum grade should be selected both for reliable operation and for good appearance. Even if only trains short enough to pull up an 8% grade will be run, if the concept were for a mainline railroad, the appearance would be Coney Island. If helpers are to be used over part of the line, the grades there should be steeper not only to give visual justification for the helpers but also to require them on long trains.

Prototype railroads compensate for the increased resistance caused by curves by reducing the grade at curves. Modelers generally select their maximum grade based on the ability of the locomotives to pull trains upgrade around a minimum radius. Nevertheless it is good practice to reduce the grade on curves.

Special-purpose tracks with very heavy grades can be installed and will function well. One possibility would be a rapid drop into a hidden yard. An actual example was an 8% grade installed to create a loop for running at public shows which connected the western end of its point-to-point layout with the eastern end on the original layout of the Summit-New Providence HO RR Club. This grade was used only for public shows and trains always went downgrade.

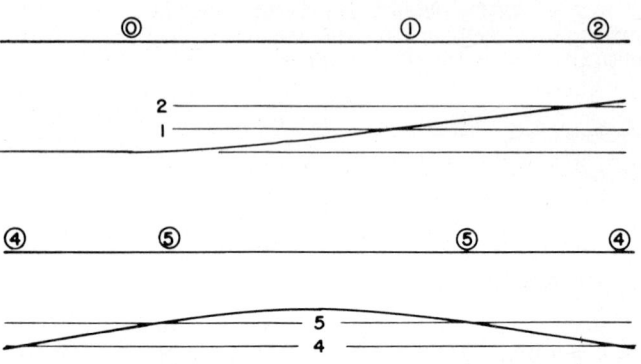

Fig. 32 Vertical curves

The vertical curves which connect level track to grades or one grade to another are usually not designed but left as a construction detail, often by bending a heavy subroadbed. They are, nevertheless, important and should be of a very large radius. Track designs should allow room for the vertical curves as illustrated in Fig. 32. It is usually sufficient to allow extra distance between the last elevation for the old grade or level track and the first elevation marker on the new grade.

Inadequate radius of vertical curves can cause false uncoupling if the type of coupler used can separate vertically (Fig. 35). No switches or other complicated trackwork should be installed on a vertical curve.

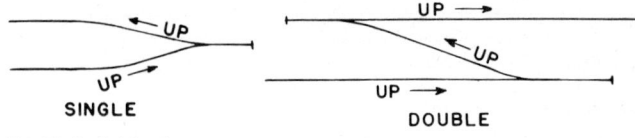

Fig. 33 Switchbacks

6.7 SWITCH BACKS

A space-saving way of gaining elevation is a switch back. Because trains must reverse and back up to continue climbing, switch backs are not suitable for long trains or important lines. A switch back consists of a stub track with a turnout as shown on the left in Fig. 33. A single switch back may be used on a switching line to reach an industry but normally they are built in pairs as the double switch-back on the right in the figure. The Lackawanna reached Ithaca via a double switch-back and the B&O passenger trains climbed from the river-level tracks to the Cleveland Union Terminal via a double switch-back. In 1974 the BN was operating into Lead, S.D. over a switch-back. Fig. 8, Chapter 11 and Fig. 10, Chapter 4 show switch backs on a model, single and double respectively. Multiple pairs of switchbacks existed on the prototype. One example was on the PRR line to Snow Shoe, Pa.

6.8 COUPLERS AND TRACK DESIGN

General

The capabilities and limitations of model couplers have great impact on track design. Exceeding the working limits of couplers will cause derailments, false uncouplings, or failures to couple. Even in scales such as N where one coupler design predominated in 1974, there were other smaller, more-nearly scale couplers available which had reduced operating capabilities. The possibility of converting to such smaller couplers at a later date should be weighed before designing tracks which press the operating limits of a larger coupler.

The limitations discussed here are inherent in the designs of couplers. These limitations cannot be overcome by a more precise adjustment. As a practical matter, however, some allowance must be made for misadjustment. The illustrations which follow assume precisely-adjusted couplers on precision cars and track.

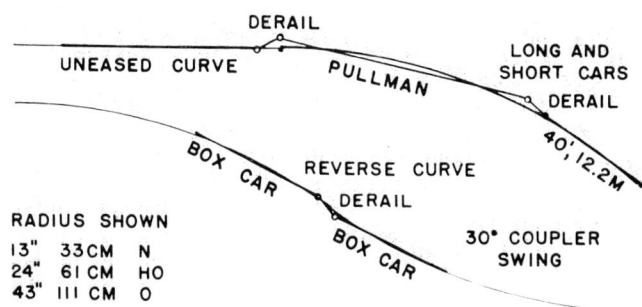

Fig. 34 Limitation of coupler swing

Coupler Swing

Regardless of type, couplers allow only a limited lateral relative motion between car ends, usually by swinging in a pocket. If that limit is exceeded, derailments are certain. Even with cars of equal length between king bolts and overhand beyond king bolts, there is a limit to the minimum radius. As shown in Fig. 34, coupled cars of unequal length or overhang beyond the trucks, cars operating from a tangent to a circular curve without an intervening easement, or operating over a reverse curve present the critical problems. If the track design does not permit trouble-free operation with all cars and locomotives, a restriction must be placed on the equipment which can be operated, a coupler with greater capabilities adopted, or the troubles simply lived with.

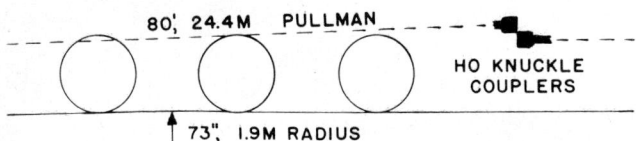

Fig. 35 False uncoupling

Vertical Tolerance

When couplers can slide apart vertically, false uncoupling can be caused by vertical curves as shown in Fig. 35 for HO knuckle couplers. Reverse vertical curves are even a greater hazard. The problem is more severe than indicated by the figure as couplers work up and down in their pockets and may part in operation even if they engage when standing.

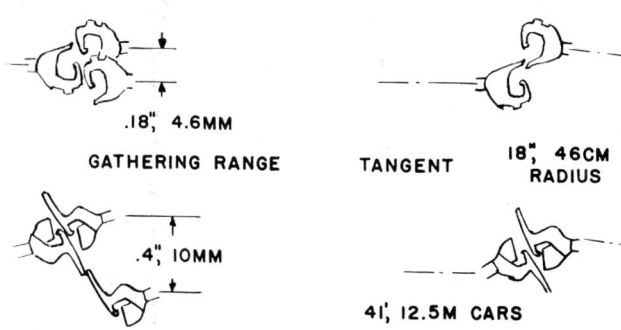

Fig. 36 Horizontal gathering range

Gathering Range

The distance one coupler can be displaced with respect to another and still couple is called *gathering range*. This range is a function of coupler design. In Fig. 36 are shown the horizontal gathering ranges of the two most popular HO couplers of 1974. The range of the coupler at the bottom is as large as has ever been available in HO, one of the objectives of the HO Standards Committee, NMRA when they developed this design in 1954.

Horizontal gathering range critically affects the design of tracks on which coupling is to take place regularly. The HO Standards Committee, NMRA found it took approximately a 1/8″ (3mm) gathering range to assure coupling in HO on straight track with cars in good but not necessarily perfect adjustment. More gathering range is required on curves as can be seen on the right in Fig. 36, for a particularly severe case. Actual performance is worse as the figure assumes perfect adjustment.

Regardless of the coupler selected at the time the layout is designed, the possibility always exists that a change will be made later to a coupler with less capabilities. A safe design rule for reliable operation is that all tracks on which coupling regularly takes place shall be straight.

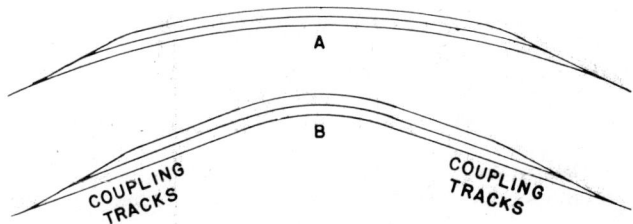

Fig. 37 Coupling tracks

Yards or spurs which must include a curve generally offer the choice of a continuous wide-radius curve as at A in Fig. 37 or of tangents separated by a shorter-radius curve as at B. Unless cars and locomotives are of essentially the same length and overhangs, it may be difficult to couple some combinations anywhere in a yard on a continuous curve. This might be a severe problem if a steam switcher cannot couple with its pilot coupler. In contrast, although it will be more difficult to couple on the shorter radius at B, it is always possible to push the cars off of the curve for coupling on the tangent. Fig. 13, Chapter 4 shows an interchange on a curve designed with coupling in mind.

Vertical gathering range is also critical and must not be exceeded. For knuckle couplers the vertical gathering range is almost twice the height of the knuckle but it can be exceeded by cars on a vertical curve as shown in Fig. 35. A safe rule is that tracks on which coupling normally takes place shall not be on either a vertical or on a horizontal curve.

6.9 CLEARANCE

For models of standard railroads, NMRA Standard minimum clearances should be observed, see Appendix I. The horizontal clearances given there are for tangent track, extra allowance must be made for car and locomotive overhang on curved track.

Overhang is a function of the equipment and the radius. Maximum outside overhang is generated by articulated locomotives. The top of Fig. 38 illustrates the nominal outside overhang of a UP Big Boy on two different radii. That figure does not make allowance for the extra overhang which could develop if the wheel flanges are not closely confined by the rails. Maximum inside overhang is generated by long and wide cars, a standard passenger car is shown at the bottom of Fig. 38. Using HO as an example, if 24" radius is used with the equipment shown, the minimum outside clearance would have to be 1⅝" and the minimum inside clearance 1⅛" to keep the same clearance as 1" provides on tangent.

Obviously a model of an industrial switching line neither must nor should make provision for such large overhangs. If large locomotives are not to be operated, or at least restricted from the short radii, as in fact they are on the prototype, clearances can be set by measuring the actual equipment to be operated while standing on the minimum radius.

Particular attention should be given where curved tracks approach through bridges, tunnels, abutments or piers. Such obstructions may be hard to move if at some later date it is discovered they are hit by large-overhang locomotives or cars. Small layouts, in particular, if they used commercial through bridges and tunnel portals, may present problems of overhang as there may not be room for a tangent before such clearance-restricting structures.

Track Centers

On the prototype, track centers as small as 13' (4m) have been used on tangent multiple-track. This corresponds to 3.25" (88mm) in O, 1.8" (45mm) in HO, and 1" (25mm) in N. Such close spacing does not allow adequate room between cars for fingers in the event of derailments. NMRA Standards call for a minimum spacing of 3.5" (89mm) for O and 1.94" (49mm) for HO. Most HO lines use 2" (51mm) centers. With the latter distance, even the largest locomotives and cars can be operated over 48" (1.2m) radius as can be verified by the data in Fig. 38. Below that radius consideration should be given to increasing the distance between track centers depending upon the equipment to be operated. On a 24" (61cm) radius with the largest equipment, HO track centers should be about 2.75" (7cm). Check the clearance required for the largest equipment which will be operated before designing parallel tracks on tight radii. Do not forget to check for overhang problems at switches.

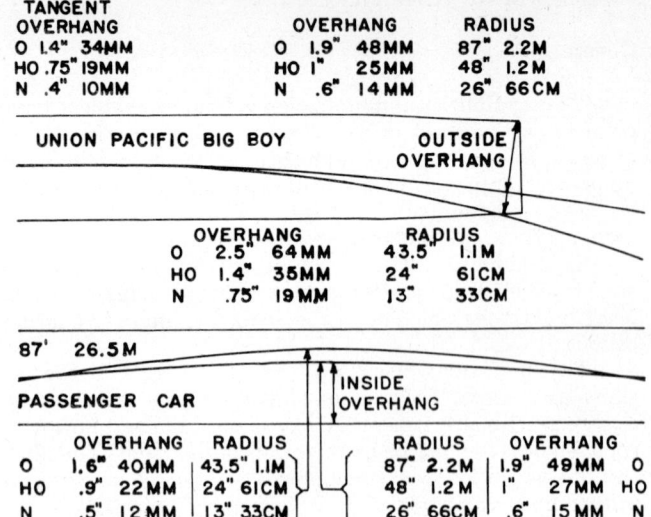

Fig. 38 Overhang on curves

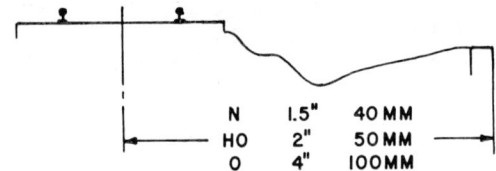

Fig. 39 Clearance to benchwork edge

Clearance to Benchwork Edge

Minimum distance from a benchwork edge is another standard which should be adopted before starting preliminary design. This distance should be great enough to permit the scenery to catch a derailed car. 1.5" (38mm) in N, 2" (5cm) in HO, and 4" (10cm) in O appear to be adequate provided the scenery is of a shape which will prevent a car from rolling over it, see Fig. 39. This is one standard which can be violated if necessary simply by providing some other form of protection such as a sheet of clear plastic extending up from the benchwork.

Benchwork on the Peninsula Model Railroad Club in California is neat, strong, functional; made mostly of 1 x 3" boards of spruce or pine and held together with screws, not nails. Gridwork makes easy the location of uprights to support subroadbed on elevated trackage and skeletal framework for scenery. Avoid use of orange crate wood for tablework.

CHAPTER 7
PRELIMINARY DESIGN

7.1 GENERAL

Preliminary design tests the proposed concept against various arrangements of track and benchwork. During this phase it is important that detailed design not be undertaken even for part of the railroad to avoid the danger of locking in on a specific feature and thus overlooking some better general approach. An exception is in critical areas where it is questionable if a specific track arrangement will fit (Fig. 9, Chapter 8).

Particularly on small layouts, the preliminary design phase should include an examination of all main-track patterns which could conceivably match both the available space and the concept. On large layouts parts of the railroad can be built independently of the rest. In fact only a portion of the final plan may be built initially. In such cases preliminary plans need be carried only to the point where it is assured that the first construction will not lead to difficult problems in later years where the railroad is expanded. Detailed planning then can start on the first portion to be constructed with the rest of the layout remaining at the preliminary design stage (Section 7.8).

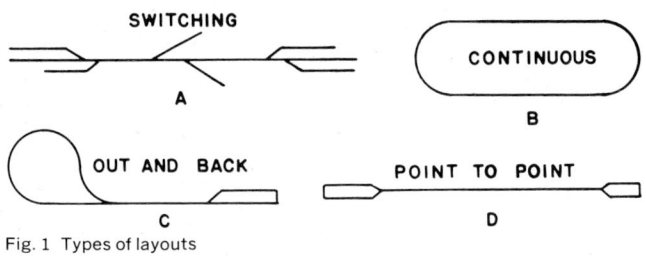

Fig. 1 Types of layouts

7.2 LAYOUT TYPES

An early decision should be the basic type of layout, switching as at A in Fig. 1, continuous as at B, out-and-back, C, or point-to-point as at D. The smallest layouts are almost forced to be either switching or continuous but even small layouts can be of the out-and-back type, (Fig. 4, Chapter 8). Point-to-point main lines are usually considered practical only for medium and large layouts but a short stub branch can be included on all but the smallest layouts (Fig. 1, Chapter 8).

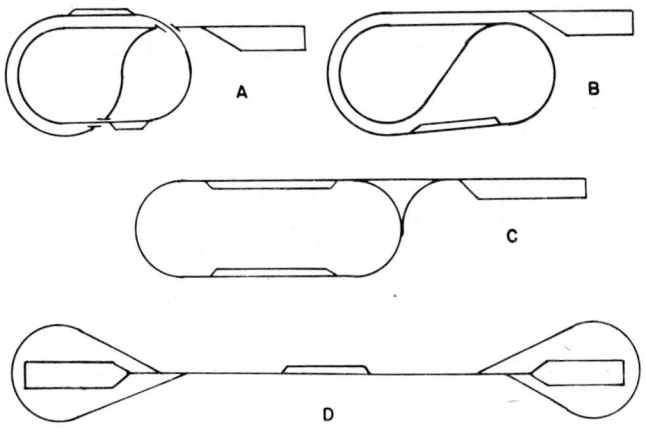

Fig. 2 Out-and-back layouts

Although a terminal can be led off of a continuous main line (Fig. 4, Chapter 8) trains must either back in or back out. If the concept is for a terminal and space is limited, one of the out-and-back possibilities shown in Fig. 2 may be the best. At A the entire main line beyond the junction is a reversing loop. A train departing the terminal passes each way station just once before returning to the terminal. At B the main line terminates in a reversing loop so a train passes each way station twice, once outbound and once returning thus remaining out of the terminal for a longer time for the same length of track. If the loop is made into another terminal, as is the loop at Bay Head Junction, N.J. on the New York & Long Branch RR, this type of layout becomes a point-to-point.

Out-and-back can be combined with continuous running as at C in Fig. 2 by placing the terminal on a wye as the prototype passenger terminal at St. Louis. A method of operation which has been used on such layouts is for each train out from the terminal to circle the loop a specific number of times and then return to the terminal. In the same vein, reversing loops may be placed at each end of a point-to-point line permitting trains to traverse the line several times before entering the other terminal as at D in Fig. 2.

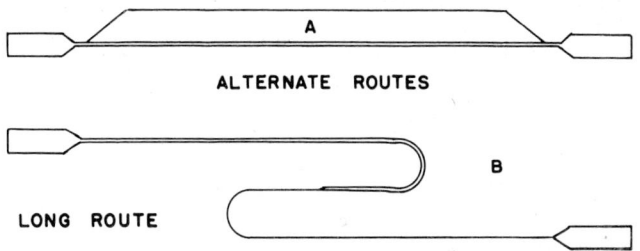

Fig. 3 Alternate vs one route

In the thirties, on layouts which had the space, a common design was to provide both a low-level main line and what was often called a 'mountain division' connecting the same two points on the layout such as at A in Fig. 3 for a point-to-point layout. However model railroads just do not have main lines adequately long. In most cases it makes for more interesting and more prototype-like operation if the two alternate routes are connected in tandem as at B in Fig. 3. When the Columbus, Ohio Model Railroad Club made such a modification to the HO layout they then had in the basement of the ex-interurban station, they found the new arrangement much better.

Although beginners tend to like layouts with alternate routes, preferably with reversing loops so the trains can run in various patterns in either direction, such running is more of a game than a duplication of the prototype. An exception would be a concept of a busy, complex interlocking. In such a case it might be helpful if a train departing the interlocking on one route could have a choice of routes to return.

7.3 PRELIMINARY BENCHWORK DESIGN

After design standards (Section 6.1) have been adopted, in most cases it is possible to conceive of several benchwork types which will fit into the available space and also conform to the standards. Fig. 4 shows three of the many possible benchworks for a 16' by 21' (4.9 by 6.4m) room with minimum-width aisles of 3' (.9m) and maximum distance from an aisle of 3' (.9m). Obviously each of the designs

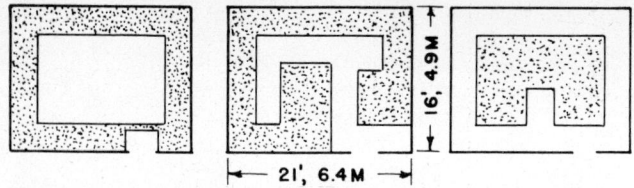

Fig. 4 Benchwork possibilities for same room

shown has advantages and disadvantages as compared to the others. There may be compelling reasons which exclude some possible designs, for example that the doorway must not be blocked. The important point is to be sure that all reasonable possibilities have been considered (Section 3.3).

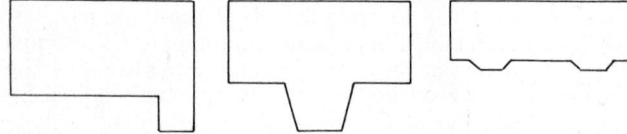

Fig. 5 Benchwork projections

Small layouts may present the designer with little choice of benchwork shape. Higher authority may edict that so much space and no more is available. In particular portable layouts may be confined to simple rectangular shapes for structural reasons when being transported. Unless so constrained, possible alternatives to simple rectangular table or benchwork should be investigated. Even small projections such as those in Fig. 5 may permit the addition of an interesting wharf scene or perhaps a small stub terminal. A small extension to the width at a crucial point may allow a critically tight main-line curve to be widened. Consideration should be given at this stage to how the railroad could be expanded if that later proves feasible (Section 7.8).

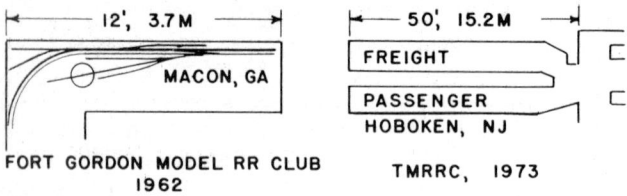

Fig. 6 Stub terminals on peninsulas

The larger the layout, the greater are the number of possibilities for benchwork designs. In most cases it becomes apparent after testing a few possibilities that certain portions of some of the designs are particularly suited to parts of the concept of the railroad. The definitive benchwork design begins to take form from those parts.

Peninsular or shelf benchworks too narrow to permit a semicircle at minimum radius are ideal for stub terminals as shown in Fig. 6. Access to all tracks is excellent and effective use has been made of the space.

Small benchwork projections can be used to advantage to add space for complex trackage to which access is critical. Fig. 13, Chapter 4, illustrates a peninsula added beside a way station for an industrial area. Fig. 7 shows a benchwork extension built for an engine terminal.

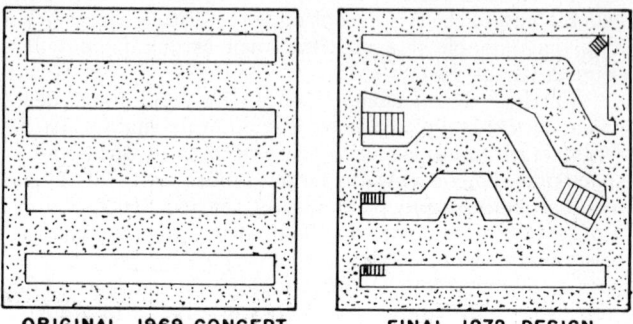

Fig. 8 Development of a benchwork plan

When easy entrance can be provided into an interior aisle, access to the tracks at large stations can be significantly improved by placing the aisle at the center of the station rather than along one side. In Fig. 7 the access aisle for Pittsburgh is between the freight and passenger facilities which allows both to be worked simultaneously without interference between operators. In Fig. 6 an aisle has been placed between the freight and passenger yards at Hoboken.

There is great interaction between preliminary benchwork and preliminary layout design. As an illustration, on the left in Fig. 8 is the original 1969 conception of rabbit-warren benchwork for the first section of the HO layout

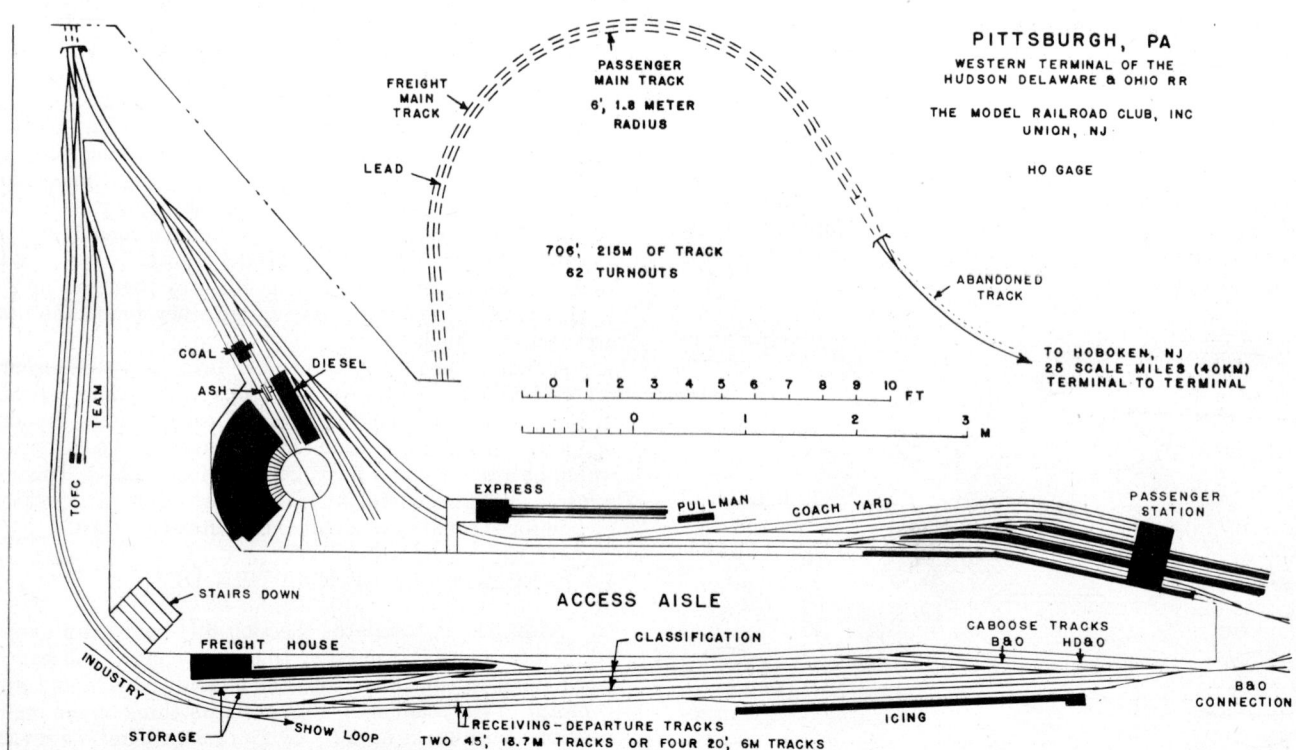

Fig. 7 Terminal using benchwork projections

Chapter 7

to be built by The Model RR Club. That benchwork followed their design rules and used the space effectively. However preliminary layout design soon disclosed that the western terminal should have a long access aisle. Therefore the benchwork design was modified as on the right in Fig. 8 to provide an L-shaped aisle for the terminal. This aisle can be seen in greater detail in Fig. 7.

7.4 PRELIMINARY LAYOUT DESIGN

General

Preliminary benchwork plans should be tested by preliminary layout designs. Early layout plans should be restricted to main tracks, sidings and significant features such as yards and major rivers. Industrial tracks and the like can be indicated in a rough manner, but drawing secondary tracks with any accuracy is not only a waste of time but also tends to obscure the overall view. The latter is of overriding importance at this stage.

Drawing Scale

Preliminary plans should always be drawn to a scale small enough that the entire layout can be viewed as a whole, not piece by piece. Small layouts certainly should have their preliminary plans drawn so they would fit a page of this book. A scale of ¼" = 1' or 50:1 is good for most HO plans.

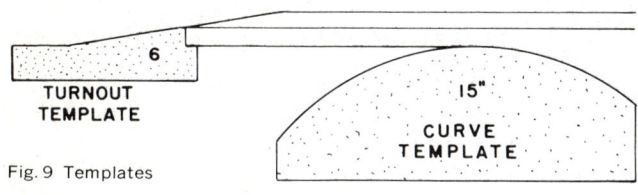

Fig. 9 Templates

Templates

Experience has shown that there is a great tendency to sketch in curves which are too sharp and ladders which are too steep if preliminary plans are drawn by eye. It is advisable to make templates for the various minimum radii and turnouts as indicated in Fig. 9, see also Fig. 19, Chapter 6 for turnout templates. The radius templates will save time as compared to locating centers and drawing the curves with a compass. Layouts to be built with prefabricated fixed-radius track such as Atlas Snap Track are best designed with special templates, see Fig. 10, Chapter 8.

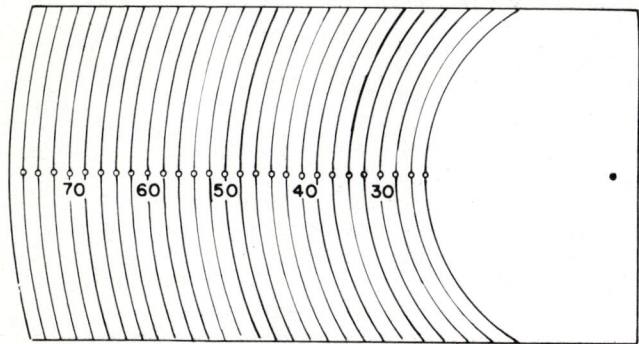

Fig. 10 Transparent curve template

Curve templates may be made from card stock but if several radii are required, a transparent template made of acetate or other plastic is convenient. The method of cutting and filling V grooves with wax shown in Fig. 20, Chapter 6 together with a string compass can be used to make a series of concentric arcs on a sheet of clear plastic with the result shown in Fig. 10. These arcs not only show how a curve fits into a plan but once the curve is fitted, its center is automatically located. The holes at the center and at various radii for pencil points permit the template to be used to draw the curve.

Grades

A careful examination of grades and vertical distance between tracks crossing must be made. Always allow ample vertical clearance in the preliminary plans. Clearances can be squeezed down to the minimum later if that becomes desirable. Fig. 11 suggests some minimum vertical spacings for use in preliminary plans. Appendix I gives the NMRA Standard Clearances.

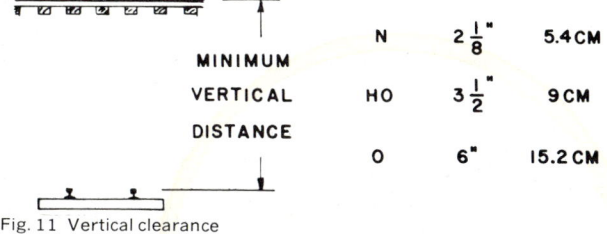

Fig. 11 Vertical clearance

Establish some standard for noting relative elevations on the plans. A common method is to place the elevation within a circle as shown in Fig. 12. This method is used in all other figures of this Handbook where elevations are included. The elevations should be indicated at the beginning and

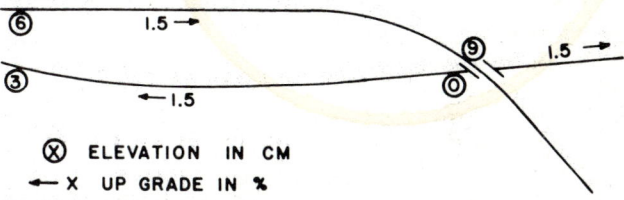

Fig. 12 Elevations and grades

ending of every grade and on both tracks at crossings. Allow room for vertical curves as explained in Section 6.6. The zero reference for elevations could be the floor or the top of the benchwork provided such a surface is dead level. Often the lowest track is designated as zero elevation as the figures then more clearly indicate the relative heights of the various tracks. Elevation notations are a good point to introduce the metric system for centimeters are a fine enough division for practical purposes and eliminate the fractions or decimals required if inches are used.

On preliminary plans it is useful to indicate the percent of grade and the direction of the grade. Adopt a convention such as that in Fig. 12 where the arrows point up grade.

Allow Leeway

It is vital to allow leeway in preliminary plans. Do not attempt to squeeze in tracks to the limits permitted by the standards. When detailed plans are drawn they have a habit of requiring a little more room here and there for things overlooked during preliminary planning. Keep the tracks a bit further from obstructions and benchwork edges than is absolutely required. Hold grades to less than the maximum, particularly on short runs. Compensate for curves by easing the grade on curves. It is always possible to go to the limits permitted later but it is difficult to make adjustments if everything is stretched initially.

Grid

After a preliminary plan is ready for detailed development, it is convenient to place an accurate grid on the drawing for reference (Section 9.5).

7.5 MAIN TRACKS AND SIDINGS

Preliminary layout design usually starts with placing the main tracks and sidings. Although many model railroaders use 'siding' in a general way, for clarity in this Handbook the terms 'main track' and 'siding' are in accordance with official prototype practice. The Western Pacific Rule

Book defined main track as, "A track extending through yards and between stations, upon which trains are operated by time-table or train orders, or both, or the use of which is governed by block signals," and siding as, "A track auxiliary to the main track for the meeting or passing of trains." Sidings may be single-ended, i.e., spur, or double-ended, i.e., returned to the main track at both ends. An auxiliary track not used for the meeting or passing of trains is not a siding and is called a side track, spur or a similar general term or by a specific name such as caboose track.

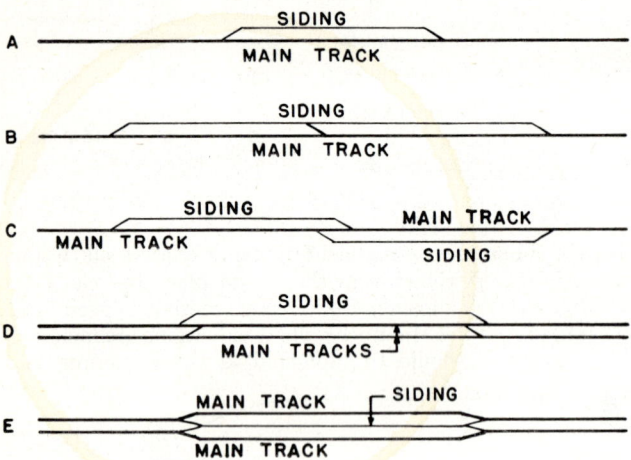

Fig. 13 Sidings

Various track possibilities should be tried by sketching in the main tracks and sidings. Fig. 1, Chapter 5 shows three different arrangements of main tracks and sidings for the same benchwork.

For most model single-track lines, the simple siding at A in Fig. 13 is adequate. Such sidings should be as long as the longest train if possible, otherwise a long train will have to saw by. When a siding is significantly longer than many of the trains, it may be convenient to arrange the siding to accept two trains. At B a crossover has been placed between the center of the siding and the main track. This, however, gives the appearance of double track and the distinction of appearance between main track and siding may be lost. By lapping the sidings as at C a better scenic effect may be achieved and the main track becomes obvious. Further, side tracks on both sides of the main track can be led from the sidings rather than some from the main track.

On double-track lines, a single siding can be made to serve both tracks. In Fig. 13 D crossovers have been placed between the main tracks and at E the siding has been placed between the main tracks. The latter is more obvious but side tracks cannot be led directly into the siding. The crossovers of Fig. 13 are used to route trains but when installed only for drilling, crossovers should be trailing if possible (Section 6.3).

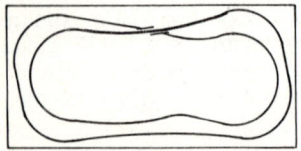 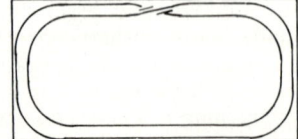

Fig. 14 Avoid parallelism

As a general rule a better effect is achieved if main tracks of different routes or of successive portions of the same route do not parallel each other or the edge of the benchwork. Fig. 14 shows the contrast of non-parallel with parallel tracks. Even if only a slight angle is possible, the improvement is noticeable (Fig. 1, Chapter 6).

Every effort should be made to prevent the track pattern from being obvious at a glance. Where space allows, two routes or successive portions of the same route should not follow each other for long distances, also the direction

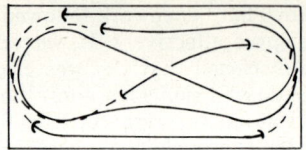 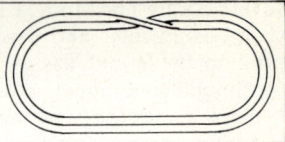

Fig. 15 Avoid an obvious track pattern

of train movement with respect to the viewer should be reversed when possible the next time the train passes through the same general area of the benchwork. Fig. 15 compares two different three-times-around folded ovals of main track.

When the control system permits, a better effect is achieved if main tracks cross from one side of the benchwork to another occasionally rather than following a single benchwork edge or access aisle. The major design limitation imposed by walkaround control is that main tracks must follow access aisles (Section 5.2).

To keep a train from reappearing quickly at the same general area, main tracks should run the maximum practical distance before returning as at the top of Fig. 16 in contrast to looping in one part of the benchwork before proceeding to the next part as at the bottom of the figure. This may be a problem for layouts designed for expansion (Section 7.8).

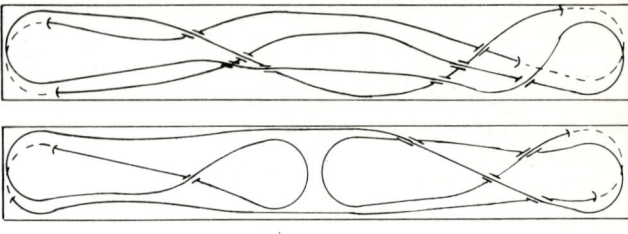

Fig. 16 Maximize runs before returning

It creates a greater illusion of distance if long stretches of tangent are broken by a curve even if slight. This must be weighed against the need to obtain maximum room in front of a track against a wall. Also long straights can be built for effect. The outstanding scenic feature, the one which is remembered by those who saw the now-dismantled HO layout of the Bayonne, N.J. Club, was its scale mile of tangent four-track main line.

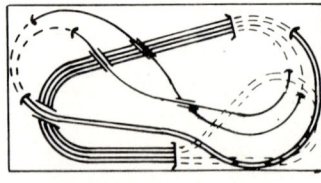

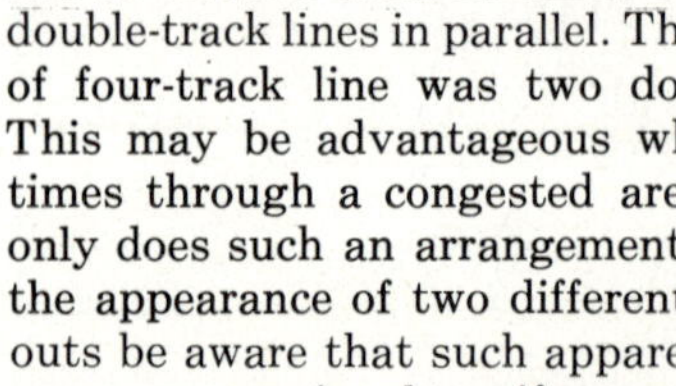

Fig. 17 Multiple-track appearance

The appearance of double or multiple-track main lines can be created even on small layouts by running single or double-track lines in parallel. The aforementioned scale mile of four-track line was two double-track lines in parallel. This may be advantageous when the line passes several times through a congested area (Fig. 5, Chapter 5). Not only does such an arrangement save space but it can give the appearance of two different railroads. On two-rail layouts be aware that such apparent multiple track might become a reversing loop if a crossover is installed (Section 5.3).

Combining lines into apparent multiple track is particularly effective on layouts whose purpose is the display of moving trains, an example is given in Fig. 17. This particular design assumes continuous running around the folded oval and the tracks are arranged for right-hand running on both the two and the four-track segments.

When the concept is for an operating railroad in contrast to one for display, combining lines for appearance reasons works against the concept in most cases.

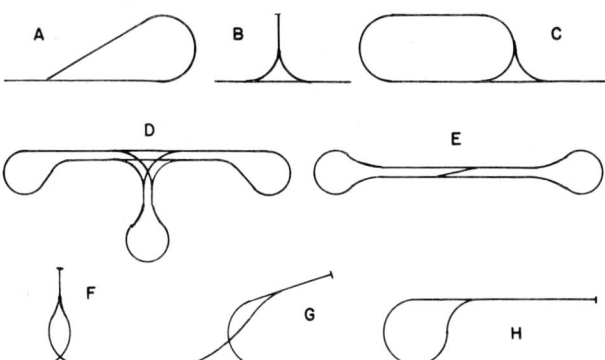

Fig. 18 Reversing tracks

7.6 REVERSING TRACKS

Reversing tracks permit the heading of a train to be reversed when the train returns over the same track.

For two-rail, reversing tracks introduce electrical problems (Section 5.3). Although electrical problems can always be solved by more complex circuits, the designer should be aware of them as a minor modification of the track plan may make a major simplification in the wiring.

The classic reversing track in model railroading is the reversing loop as at A in Fig. 18. Beginners often add such loops merely to provide alternate running paths. However, if the objective is to create a scale railroad, reversing tracks of any sort should have a purpose, for example to turn the piggy-back cars for unloading at an end-ramp TOFC terminal.

The second common reversing track is a wye such as at B in Fig. 18. However, if the track from the wye is not stub but continuous, a wye and a reversing loop become one and the same, C in the figure. Going around a wye requires a backing movement, going around a loop does not. That is the distinction made in this Handbook.

Not all track which appears to be a reversing loop or a wye is such. For example the tracks at D in Fig. 18 do not include reversing tracks. What appears to be double track is, electrically for two-rail, two single tracks going in opposite directions. Putting a crossover between such tracks as at E introduces a reversing loop which must be so wired.

Wyes can be compressed or bent to fit available space. At F is a wye with a crossing of the type built by the NYC at Rochester. Such a wye can be bent as at G. Model examples can be seen in Figs. 22 and 24. It is even possible to eliminate one switch of a wye as shown at H. Fig. 8, Chapter 2 shows a home layout with three reversing tracks of this type.

7.7 CROSSOVERS AND LADDERS

Crossovers

A crossover is two turnouts and a connecting track to permit a train to crossover from one parallel track to another. If provided for only one direction of travel it is called a single crossover as on the left in Fig. 19. That crossover, for right-hand running, is called a facing crossover. For left-hand running it would be a trailing crossover. Crossovers installed for switching moves only and not to route trains should be trailing wherever possible to reduce derailment hazard.

If both a trailing and a facing crossover are installed in close proximity, the combination is called a double crossover as at the center of Fig. 19. Where space is critical, the two crossovers can be overlaid as on the right to form a scissors crossover. When using prefabricated turnouts and crossings without modification, it is usually necessary to increase track centers for scissors crossovers (Fig. 11, Chapter 8).

See Section 6.2, Reverse Curves, for precautions concerning the design of crossovers.

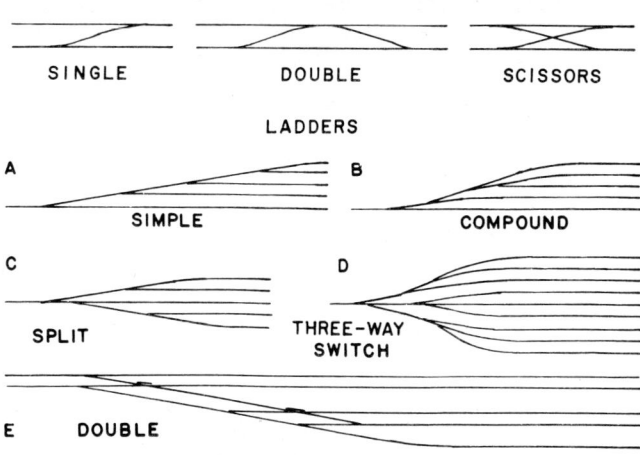

Fig. 19 Ladders and crossovers

Model railroaders typically call the track configurations shown under crossovers in Fig. 19 just that regardless of their location as did the prototype in the past. Technically, on the prototype today, the term crossover has a more restricted meaning.

Ladders

Ladders are the tracks and switches connecting the ends of parallel (body) tracks such as those in yards. Where space permits, the easiest to build and most reliable is the simple ladder shown at A in Fig. 19. It is important when sketching a ladder, even on the preliminary plans, that a template or other accurate means of drawing the frog angle be used as there is a tendency to draw the ladders too steeply and thus create problems during final design.

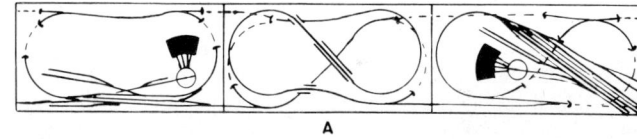

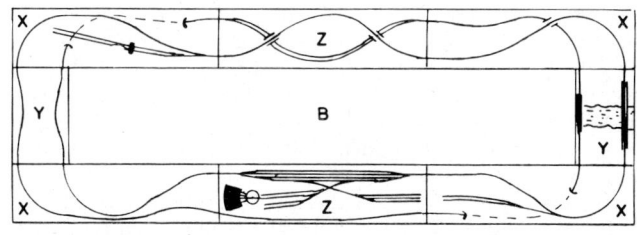

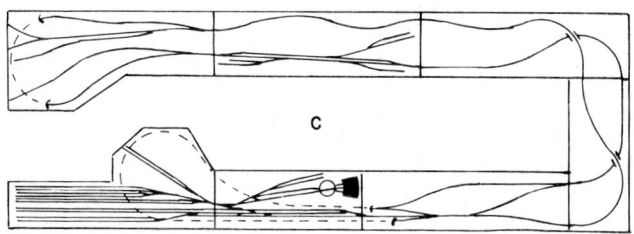

Fig. 20 Modular design

Chapter 7   37

If a simple ladder does not permit the yard tracks to be long enough, a compound ladder, Fig. 19 B or a split ladder, C, will save space, the split ladder being preferred if it is appropriate. One or both parts of the split ladder can be compound if even more space must be saved. The three-way switch ladder at D is the shortest but is not used on the prototype except for hump yards.

Passenger stations in particular may install a double ladder with slip switches as at E to permit simultaneous moves on the ladder. In Chapter 10, see Fig. 10 for a prototype example of double and triple ladders and Fig. 11 for a double ladder on a model.

7.8 DESIGN FOR EXPANSION

General

It is vital that the size of the layout designed should not exceed the capabilities of the available manpower for construction, operation, and particularly for maintenance. However those limits may not be known in the beginning. One solution is to design a layout clearly within the capabilities of its builders but to provide for its expansion later if that proves feasible.

There are other reasons to design for expansion. Among them are when more space may become available later or the layout may have to be moved, also for portable layouts which will be set up in different areas.

Modular Design

A layout can be designed as a series of modules, expansion taking place by adding more modules. Three of the possible modular approaches are shown in Fig. 20.

By building with standardized locations of interconnecting tracks, portable layouts which are complete in themselves can be brought together to form a large railroad as illustrated at the top of Fig. 20. This technique is well suited to organizations such as Divisions of an NMRA Region which might bring their portable layouts together at a convention.

The modules may not be complete railroads in themselves, the center layout of Fig. 20 requires four X modules to form a folded oval layout. The layout can be expanded by adding Y and Z modules to suit the space available. If enough standardization of interface between modules is specified, any combination of Y and Z modules could be placed in series to make a long layout in either direction.

A variation of the above technique can be applied to more permanent railroads as illustrated at the bottom of Fig. 20. If the layout is to be enlarged, new modules are designed specifically for the space. A practical example was the HO layout built in New York City by the Bell Laboratories Model RR Club. After being completed it was moved to a larger room and new modules built. Later it was transferred to Holmdel, N.J. and again new modules were built.

For all types of modular design, the number of tracks between modules should be kept to the minimum and, preferably, they should cross module boundries at near 90°. These rules have been observed in Fig. 20.

Added Lines

When space is not limiting, it is possible to use a large area for a relatively small amount of track. Only the first track to be built need be designed in detail. Expansion tracks can be shown just by general location and elevations. In this way rights of way for possible future tracks will be reserved. This technique is most applicable to point-to-point layouts. Operation can start just as soon as two stations are built and connected. The line then is extended as time and manpower permit.

Actually this is the way the prototype railroads were built.

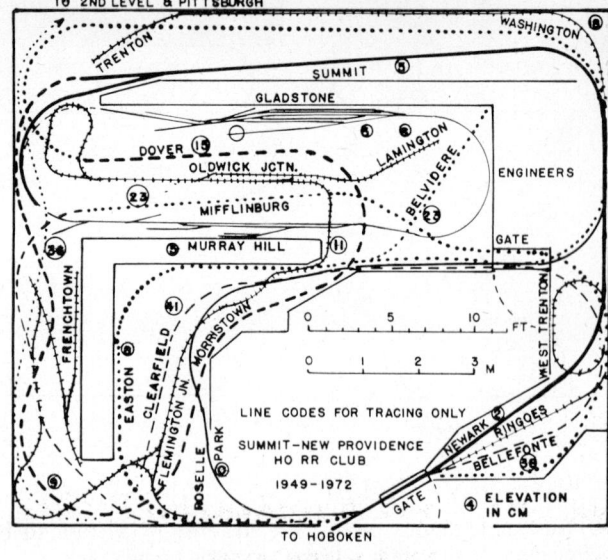

Fig. 21 Planned expansion by extending lines

Fig. 21 gives an actual example of this technique. When the club was founded in 1949 a space 30' by 36' (9.1 by 11m) was made available temporarily pending the finding of permanent quarters. Since it was not known how long finding permanent space would take, a concept for a relatively large point-to-point railroad with a possible total of over 3,000' (914m) of HO track was adopted. The preliminary plans set the routes and elevations for all the lines which might be

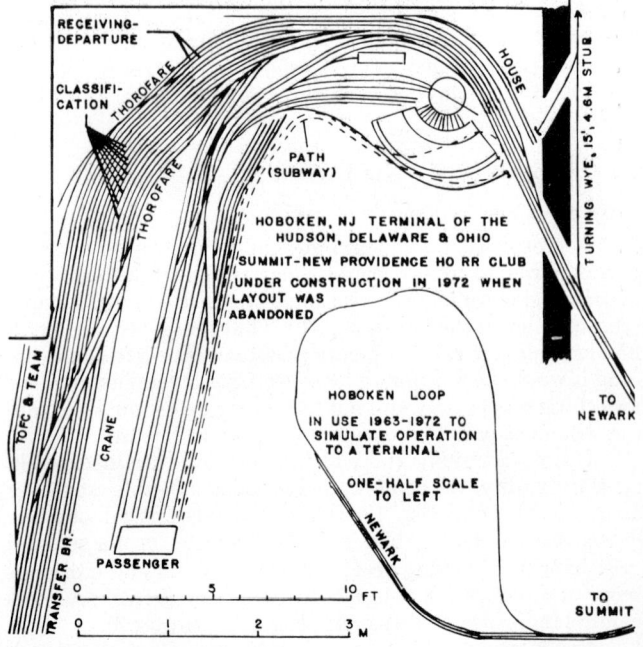

Fig. 22 Single-station expansion

38

Chapter 7

built as shown in the plan of Fig. 21. In this way space would be reserved for all tracks ever to be built and there would be no problems of interference between lines. However detailed planning was completed initially only for Gladstone and Murray Hill as these were to be the first stations built. Time table operation with waybills started in 1951 on the two station loop shown in detail on the plan and in the 1951 diagram. Benchwork was built and the line extended only as required by a growing need for more operator positions. An intermediate stage of construction is shown by the 1959 diagram as well as the final stage reached at the end of the 23-year temporary period. The club then moved to its permanent layout, Fig. 23.

The sequence of construction indicated in Fig. 21 had two major flaws. One was that the tracks nearest the aisles were built first which made it all but impossible to add scenery which would not be destroyed as the rear tracks were laid. The other was that the line was started on a branch and built toward its major terminals. As a result even after 22 years there was no terminal adequate for a layout of this size.

Expansion by Area

When a large space is available, it may be best to design a complete railroad using only a portion of the area but with provision for expansion onto new benchwork if the original layout proves too small. The author knows of two clubs on Army posts which failed primarily because they attempted to fill large areas which had been made available to them.

An expansion area can be used to add a single major feature. Fig. 22 shows an HO terminal with 750' (229m) of track designed as an expansion area for the layout shown in Fig. 21. The tunnels had been drilled through the 12" (30cm) masonry walls but only the approach tracks and wye had been built when the layout was abandoned in 1972. Pending construction of this terminal, a branch line had been connected back on the main line to form the 1.5 scale mile (2.5 scale km) reversing loop shown at the lower right which was used to simulate a terminal for the purposes of operation.

In Fig. 22 only a single line was extended into the expansion area. This is the simplest method and possibly the

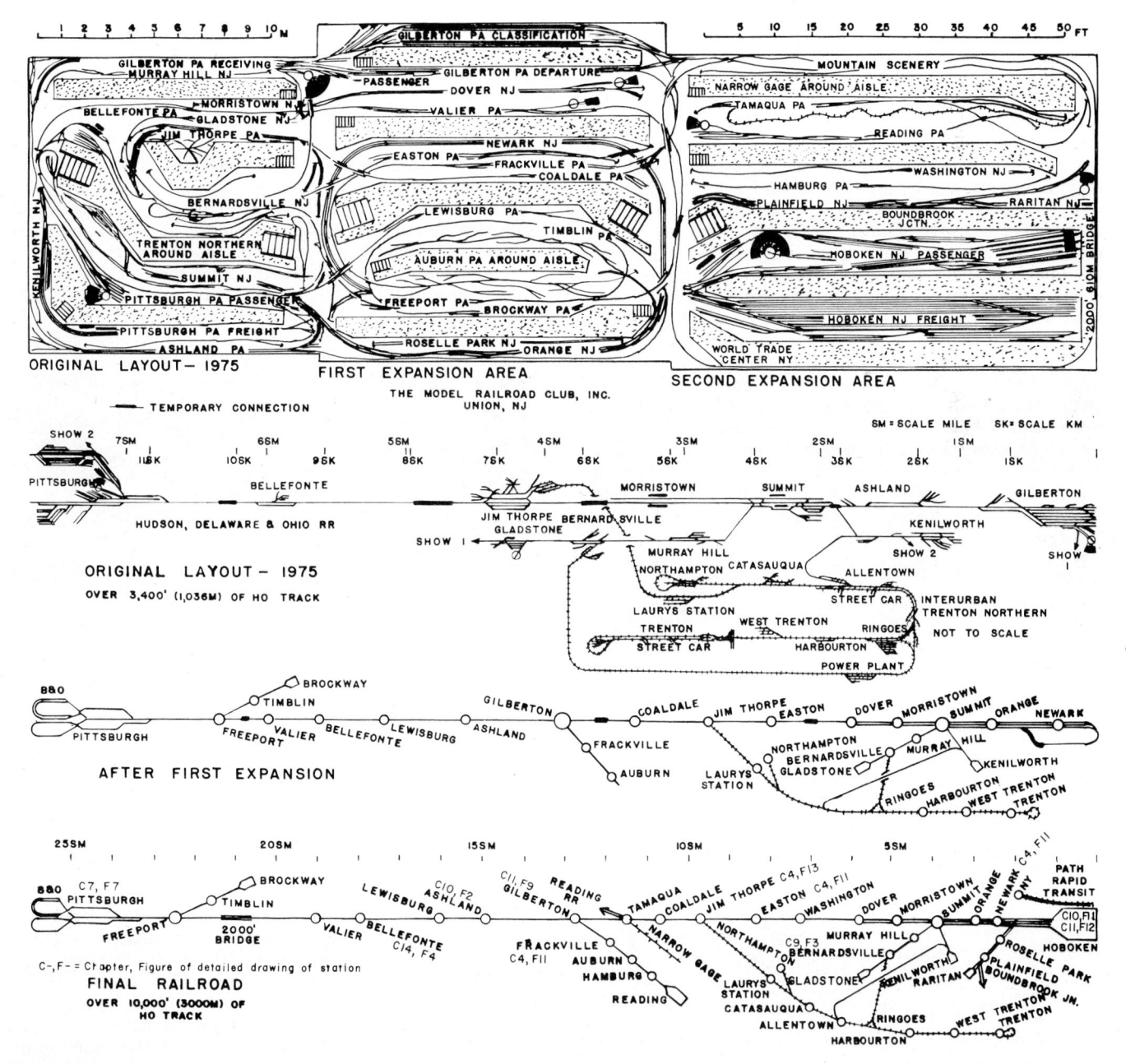

Fig. 23 Expansion by area

Chapter 7

best if the new area is separated visually from the old. However, if the layout is in an open room where the engineers and spectators can see the trains regardless of their location, there is merit in designing so that trains move the entire length of the expanded layout before returning. Thus they will not reappear in the same general area quickly. The cost is temporary tracks which must be built to make a complete railroad at each stage of expansion. Such temporary tracks may, when the layout is expanded, become industrial tracks, remain to form show loops, be reconnected as part of another line, or be abandoned.

Fig. 23 shows an extremely large HO railroad designed for construction in three stages. The building for this layout was designed especially for the purpose and the expansion areas represent future building extensions. The railroads for each of the three stages of construction are shown in the diagrams under the plan. Only the first section, something over 3,400′ (1,036m) of track, had been designed in detail by 1974 and that fact is reflected in the plan and diagrams of Fig. 23. Construction of the first section was well along in 1974.

7.9 TRACK DIAGRAMS

A well worked-out concept normally includes an assumed map of the proposed railroad as in Fig. 2, Chapter 2. Such a map shows the sequence of stations but, except for simple track patterns such as a continuous oval once around the benchwork, it is difficult to keep the railroad precisely in mind as it is designed. Therefore it is good practice to draw a track diagram of the railroad and keep it current. A diagram is actually a stretched-out version of the track plan although usually the width is to a different scale than the length in order to show clearly parallel tracks, crossovers, etc. As an example, Fig. 24 is the end result of the preliminary planning for a medium-size layout. The plan shows how the railroad would be built but the diagram above it shows more clearly how it was to be operated. The diagram also indicates how much of the railroad was included on the show loop.

The diagram of Fig. 24 follows the usual practice of drawing the track in the clearest possible manner rather than holding to a strict scale. For example the distance between Atlanta and Union Point is short compared to the scale used for the Atlanta terminal. In contrast, the diagrams of Fig. 23 are drawn to a fixed scale of length as indicated by the scale mile and kilometer marks. Such diagrams show the relationships of distances between stations to the length of the stations.

Some modelers in preparing diagrams prefer to indicate tracks crossing above or below the track at that point on the diagram, possibly even showing the vertical separation distance. Others, including the author, feel such information not only makes the diagrams more difficult to read but is better obtained from the plans.

7.10 ELEVATION DIAGRAM

Another useful diagram is an elevation, also called a profile. Fig. 25 is an example showing the elevations of the railroad (but not of the interurban) of Fig. 24. To indicate clearly small differences in elevation, the vertical scale is much larger than the horizontal scale. The rectangles above and below the grade line follow Henry T. Wilhelm's practice of indicating the clearance to tracks crossing over or under at that point.

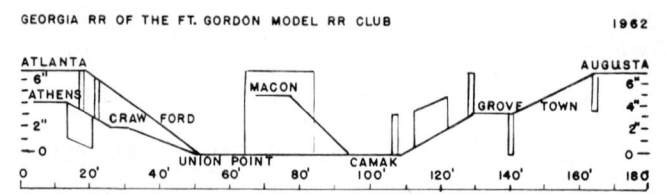

Fig. 25 Elevation diagram

7.11 SHOW LOOPS

Layouts designed to be operated in the prototype manner often are point-to-point with no tracks permitting continuous running included in the concept. This is true of the railroads shown in Figs. 21, 23, and 24. If such layouts are displayed to the public, experience has shown it is best if a connection is added which allows for the continuous running of trains. The public is primarily interested in seeing trains move. Switching of trains is desirable but only as an addition to continuous running. If the layout is large enough, two separate loops are better than one, so running can continue even if trouble develops on one loop or a train derails.

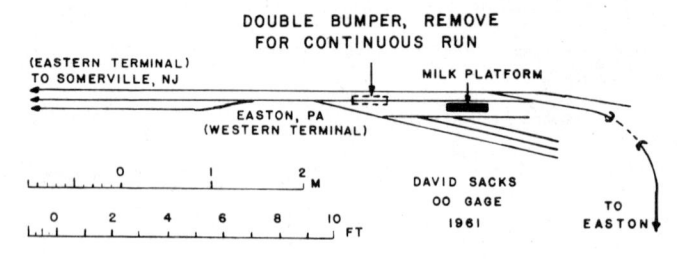

Fig. 26 Show-loop connection

By including them in the preliminary planning, show loops usually can be implemented with a minimum amount of added track. In Fig. 24 a simple crossover marked 'SHOW' connects virtually the entire main line into an oval. In Fig. 23 two show loops, SHOW 1 and SHOW 2, have been provided for the initial stage of layout construction. The track added for show loops may just stand idle during the rest of the year or perhaps be used as spurs. An example of the latter is given in Fig. 26. A double-faced bumper was placed as indicated when continuous-loop operation was not desired. The Reading had many double-faced bumpers at its West Trenton coach yard.

Leaving show loops as an item to be added later may introduce difficulties. For example the preliminary design for the layout of Fig. 21 made no provision for continuous operation for, in 1949, public shows were not contemplated. Starting in 1960, public shows were held with the trains being turned at the existing terminals. It quickly became obvious that the public did not appreciate the relative inaction of running locomotives around the train and changing the

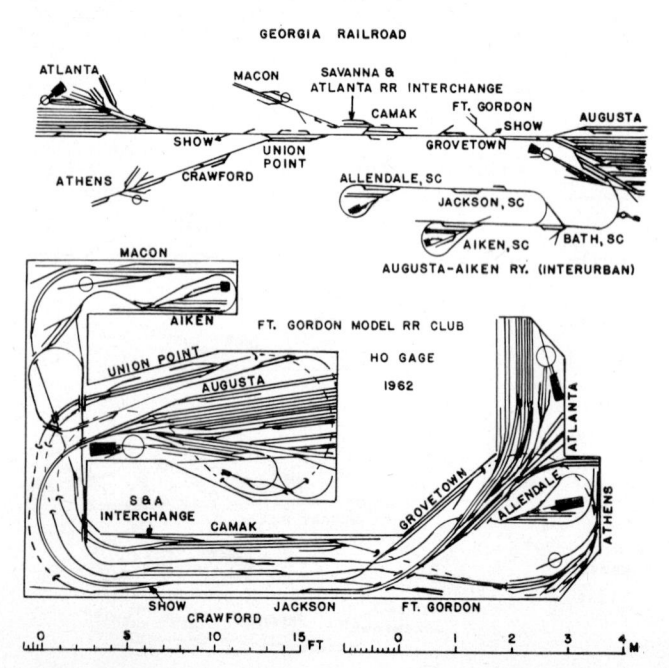

Fig. 24 Diagram for layout plan

caboose even when switchers were stationed at each terminal to speed such operation. To meet the wishes of the visitor, the then western terminal, Easton, was connected by temporary track to Flemington Jct. on the traction line and the Hoboken Loop, Fig. 22 installed. This created a continuous oval using all lines operational at that date. Later the quasi-stub switch on gantlet track shown in Fig. 28, Chapter 6 was installed to eliminate temporary track but operating show trains over the 18" (46cm) radius of the interurban was restrictive.

Finally the railroad was extended to Clearfield and an 8% down-grade track was built to return trains to the main line at Newark. The experience of this layout clearly shows the importance of designing show loops into the layout at the very beginning of planning if continuous operation is not otherwise possible.

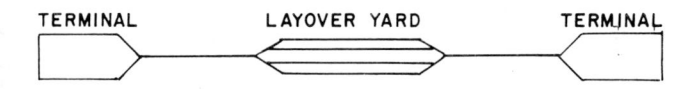

Fig. 27 Layover yard

7.12 LAYOVER TRACKS AND HIDDEN YARDS

With some concepts and methods of operation it may be an advantage to hide trains for short to extended intervals. Particularly on small layouts with the single-station concept it is helpful if a departing train does not return immediately so another train can be worked in the station. The opposite side of the oval can have holding tracks concealed behind the backdrop or in a tunnel (Fig. 1, Chapter 8).

A layover track or yard can be used to extend the apparent run on point-to-point or out-and-back layouts. In Fig. 27 a four-track layover yard is at the midpoint of the line between two terminals. Trains departing from either terminal are run into the yard and only later move on to the other terminal. This type of operation does not lend itself to conventional cab control in which one engineer controls a train for its entire run. It is, however, well suited to pass-the-buck and similar types of control as it provides a convenient location to transfer control. Layover yards of this type need not be hidden and, in fact, will be interesting to visitors if in the open.

Hidden yards or reversing loops can be used to simulate a foreign railroad interchanging with the railroad actually modeled, an example is the B&O triple-track loop in Fig. 23. In Fig. 8, Chapter 11, tracks behind the backdrop accept and return cars to and from the Sage Falls Paper Co. interchange.

A method of building a larger railroad in a given space is to install a hidden yard and operate it just as though it were visable and completely sceniced. The aptly-named Hyde yard and station, the largest on the Pacific Southern, Rocky Hill, N.J., is directly below another yard and station.

Hidden yards sometimes serve as convenient locations for rearranging trains by hand or by informal switching. In such cases they may be referred to as 'fiddle' yards. Such yards also serve as a place to store excess equipment or to store all equipment during a work session without the necessity of physically removing cars and locomotives from the track. If covered, protection is afforded against dust. The Central Jersey Model RR Association had a yard in its shop.

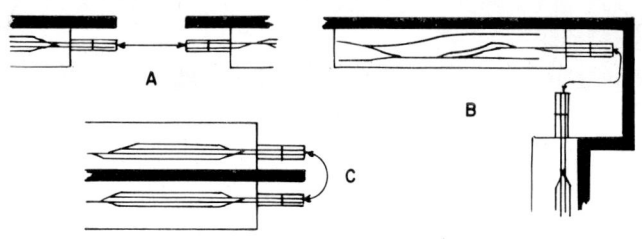

Fig. 28 Operating car floats

7.13 CAR FERRIES AND FLOATS

Railroad car ferries are self-powered track-equipped vessels. Car floats are similarly-equipped barges. Even if non-working, they and their necessary docking facilities make interesting models and serve as a logical destination for all types of freight cars, even passenger cars.

Car floats are usually, perhaps always, for freight-car service, often within a single harbor. In the case of the CRR-NJ Bronx Terminal (Fig. 1, Chapter 11) floats were the only means of access. This was true of several terminals in New York City. In the same harbor, floats were used to interchange cars among railroads. Perhaps the outstanding example was the dense float traffic between the Pennsylvania RR and the New Haven via Long Island. The Milwaukee still (1974) uses car floats to connect its detached lines on the Olympic Peninsula in Washington with the rest of its system.

Car ferries were often large such as those used for interchange service across Lake Michigan, even sea-going as in the case of Sea Train. In the past there were many examples of car ferries handling passenger cars, even entire passenger trains with their locomotives. The Texas & Pacific ferry across the Mississippi was an example. In other cases only through sleepers were placed on the ferry.

Most model car float or ferry terminals serve simply as a destination for cars, (Fig. 12, Chapter 11). In such cases it is important that a float yard large enough to hold all the cars likely to be sent to that destination be designed into the layout. Such holding tracks represent prototype practice as at the transfer bridge of the Hoboken Shore (Fig. 6, Chapter 2).

Tracks on land are connected to floats or ferries by flexible bridges called transfer bridges, float bridges, or aprons depending on the railroad or section of the country. Transfer bridges make interesting models in their own right. Even if the model car float or ferry is operating, since it normally is (or can be made to be) firm in its position when docked, the transfer bridge does not have to be adjustable for tides, listing, and other variations faced by the prototype.

Working car ferries have been built. Most have connected two transfer bridges on the same benchwork. A fine example by Richard C. Patterson operated on rails at the bottom of a water-filled river. The passage of his ferry required the opening of a draw bridge.

Because car ferries or floats can be precisely and securely aligned and attached to a transfer bridge, they do not introduce the operating problems associated with opening sections of a layout. Further they can turn on very tight radii. Consequently working car ferries or floats can be used to cross a doorway or aisle which cannot be blocked as at A in Fig. 28. They could give access to benchwork which otherwise could not be used as effectively as at B. Also they could provide rail access to benchwork in another room as at C. The more remote the detached benchwork segment is, the more useful this technique becomes just as on the prototype.

Chapter 8
DESIGN OF SMALL LAYOUTS

8.1 GENERAL

Small layouts, as defined in this Handbook, are those for which space limitations require the entire layout to be designed as a single unit. On small layouts a major change in the location of one main track usually causes the relocation of all other tracks. This is in contrast with medium and large layouts where changes can be made at one location essentially independently of other parts. Another typical characteristic of small layouts is that the minimum radius is set by the space available rather than by access requirements. Usually the minimum radius selected will confine main tracks to a limited number of positions and often the minimum radius essentially will be the only radius used. In the latter case prefabricated fixed-radius sectional track often can be used without restricting design.

Limited space is most effectively used to create a single operating feature. Therefore the concept should be simple, e.g., a small main-line station *or* an industrial switching line, not both.

In the preliminary design phase it is important to consider all reasonable main-track patterns which fit both the concept and the space. Once a preliminary design has been selected, normally only minor modifications of main tracks can be made. But, as a detail change at one point may affect other parts, some detailed planning must go hand-in-hand with preliminary planning.

After the concept and the general position of main tracks have been established, the design of small layouts becomes simpler than that of large layouts. There is less track and the number of possibilities is lower. For the final stage of design, the techniques described in Chapter 9 are as applicable to small layouts as they are to medium and large ones.

8.2 CONTINUOUS RUN

Types of Ovals

If moving trains (in contrast to switching operations) are included in the concept, for example on a layout for the purpose of displaying trains in motion, a continuous oval is virtually a must. Small layouts just cannot support adequately point-to-point operation although, if the concept is for operation at a small terminal, an out-and back loop is a possibility.

Even in a small space there are several types of ovals possible. All should be considered to assure that the one which best matches the concept is selected. Strive to keep the track pattern from being obvious at a glance.

Single-Station Operation

An excellent concept for a small layout is to utilize all available space to represent just one station. The oval, folded or otherwise, is provided merely so trains can arrive and depart from that station. Running around the oval is not a feature. This type of layout can be very realistic as, when visiting a prototype station, all that can be observed is the activity on the local tracks. Departing trains simply disappear down the track and arriving trains appear. Where they are coming from or going to is not important to the activity at the station.

So that departing trains do not immediately reappear at the other end of the station, provision can be made to hold one or more trains on the opposite side of the oval. On the left in Fig. 1 a dividing backdrop conceals a small holding yard from the station area. If desired the tracks to the rear of this backdrop can be made into a completely separate scene. (Fig. 1, Chapter 4).

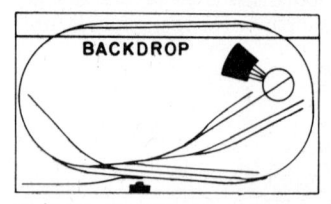

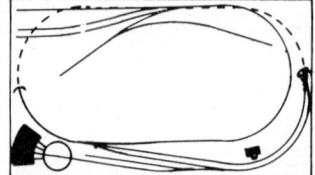

Fig. 1 Single-station layouts

A variation of the single-station theme is on the right in Fig. 1. In this case the opposite side of the main line is hidden in a tunnel. Should there be a holding yard in this tunnel, be sure the switches are readily accessible for maintenance (Section 6.3). The space above the tunnel can be used for static scenery or, as indicated in Fig. 1, for an industrial area, perhaps even a small branch-line terminal.

Layouts of this type lend themselves to the use of mirrors to extend the tracks visually beyond the edge of the benchwork (Fig. 23, Chapter 4).

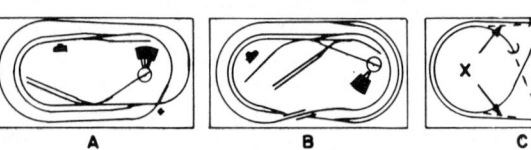

Fig. 2 Twice-around main tracks

Twice-Around Main Tracks

If a part of the concept is to keep moving trains in view in addition to the activities at a station, generally a better effect is obtained if the oval is more than just a simple once-around-the-benchwork type. Fig. 2 shows three folded-oval arrangements which have been widely used for such a purpose. At A all the tracks are at the same level with a grade crossing. The crossing provides the opportunity for the scenic and operational interests of a small interlocking plant with its attendant signals.

The layout at B in Fig. 2 is similar to that at A except that the grade crossing has been replaced by a grade separation. Advantage can be taken of the visual separation of the tracks by their difference in elevation to add a second small station with a siding so two trains can run in opposing directions.

The folded dog-bone layout at C in Fig. 2 gives the appearance of double track on its left side, a reasonable length of run, and the possibility of the two reversing loops marked X. Reversing loops of this type where the track which can be assigned solely to the loop section is short must have special wiring for two-rail (Section 5.3).

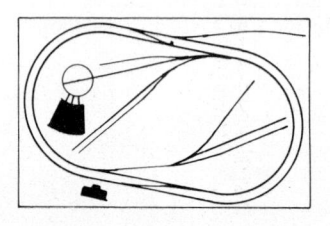

Fig. 3 Double track

Leads

To permit continuous running of one train while another locomotive is drilling in the station requires that a switching lead be provided at the station. Such a lead exists at B in Fig. 2. Alternatively a double-track oval can be installed as in Fig. 3 and the inner track used either for switching or for a second train on a continuous run. Unless there is a specific reason for modeling double track on a small layout such as wanting to run the longest possible trains, it is better to choose a single-track design. Multiple-track lines always look shorter than single track of the same length, cut down on the room for scenery, and are operationally far less interesting.

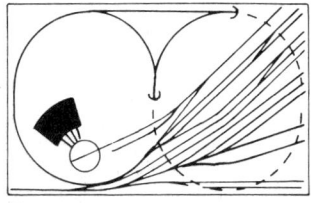

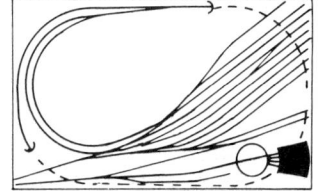

Fig. 4 Layouts with terminals

Terminals

It is possible to model a reasonable terminal on a small layout provided most of the available space is devoted to the terminal. On the left in Fig. 4 operation from the terminal is out-and-back but a continuous oval has been provided on the lower level if it is desired to keep a train in continuous motion. On the right the terminal leads from the oval so the trains in one direction have to back into the terminal and trains in the other direction have to back out. There were many examples on the prototype of through passenger trains pulling in then backing out or vise-versa but usually from a wye.

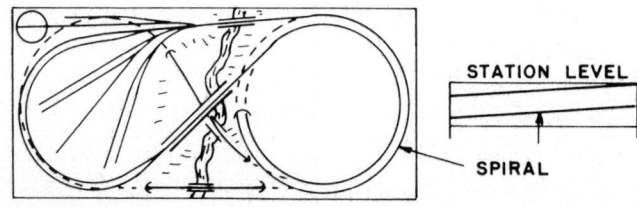

Fig. 5 Spiral layout

The suggestion has been published that two-level layouts of the general type shown on the left in Fig. 4 or at C in Fig. 2 could gain a greater vertical separation of the two levels of track by spiraling up in the manner of a cork screw. This would open up some scenic possibilities in the way of gorges and high bridges. Fig. 5 shows one possibility in which the upper tracks of the spiral are directly over the lower. This makes for more difficult construction than if they were offset.

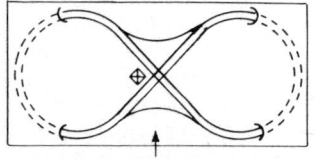

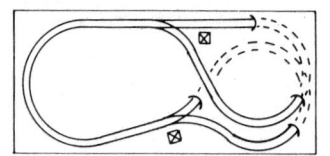

Fig. 6 Interlockings

Interlocking Plant

If trains in motion are to be featured rather than switching, an interlocking plant offers operating as well as scenic interest. At the left of Fig. 6 the scenery has been arranged so two double-track lines appear to cross at grade. The interchange tracks between these two presumably-different railroads permit the sequence of trains to be changed but are not reversing loops. Further operational interest could be obtained by constructing a small interchange yard in the space indicated. This yard would permit changing the consist of trains. Proper signals, particularly if working, add greatly to the appearance of a layout of this type. Information on interlocking signals may be found in the reference cited in Section 5.1.

On the right in Fig. 6 two diverging-route junction interlockings are simulated. The loops on the ends can be used to change the sequence of trains but are not reversing loops so signals need be provided only for one direction of travel on each track. For an interlocking tower at a single-track crossing, see Fig. 2A.

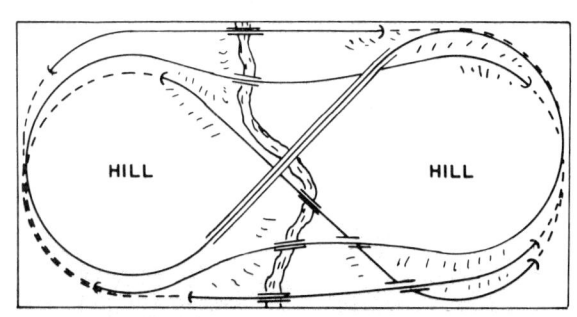

Fig. 7 Continuous run

Display of Moving Trains

If the layout is primarily or solely for the display of moving trains without requiring much operator attention, the most contorted folded-oval possible for the space probably is the best choice. Layouts of this type have been constructed frequently as portable display units for it is important that the track pattern not be obvious at a glance. This means a winding route and judicious use of tunnels and cuts to take the train from view. Fig. 7 is an example of such a design. The scenery is basically a valley between two hills. The highest level of track crosses this valley on a long trestle which is the center of scenic interest. Fig. 9, Chapter 4 is a photograph of a portable TT layout using this form of scenery. This layout has been converted to N gage. See Figs. 16, 17, and 18 of Chapter 3 for details of its benchwork.

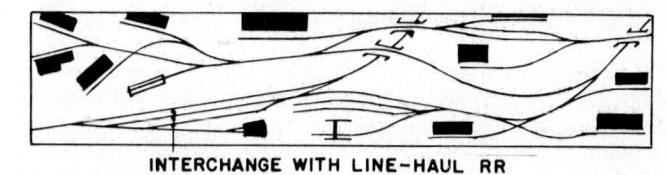

Fig. 8 Switching line

8.3 SWITCHING LINE

Far more operational interest can be built into a small area by modeling some sort of a switching line, as in an industrial area, than in modeling any type of main-line operation. Prototype switching lines are characterized by tight curves and special trackwork to get short spurs into difficult locations. No loop of any type is needed so even a narrow shelf is suitable for a switching line. Fig. 8 is an example of such a layout. However the design of a switching line is no different on a small layout than on a large so information on this subject is contained in Chapter 11.

8.4 SPECIAL RAILROADS

The layouts shown thus far in this Chapter have been based on modeling standard gauge railroads in the minimum practical area, about 5' by 9' (1.5 by 2.7m) in HO or 2'9" by 4'11" (.8 by 1.5m) in N if a loop is included. However by modeling a prototype which had tight radii, for example traction, narrow gauge, mining or logging railroads, reasonable layouts can be built in even smaller spaces or, if built on the same size benchwork which would be required for a standard-gauge line, they might not even fit the definition given for a small layout (Chapter 14).

8.5 DETAILED DESIGN OF SMALL LAYOUTS

Although on medium and large layouts detailed design should not be started until after preliminary design has led to the selection of the desired basic plan, on a small layout space is so tight that it may be necessary to check in a detailed way if some particular preliminary plan can be considered. For example in Fig. 9 the small-scale preliminary plan on the left shows a siding starting at A. It is not clear whether the dimensions of the benchwork combined with the minimum radius adopted will permit an ordinary straight turnout to be installed at this point. A large-scale drawing of that portion of the layout as shown on the right will disclose the necessary information.

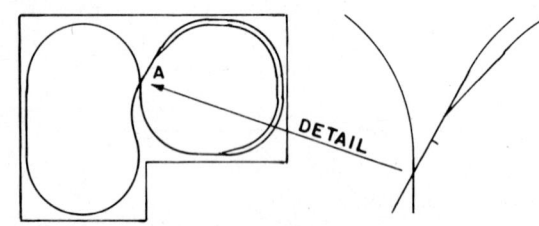

Fig. 9 Detailed check of critical point

The techniques described in Chapter 9, Final Design, are as applicable to the detailed planning stage of small layouts as they are to larger layouts.

As there is little room on small layouts to make adjustments when constructing the railroad, great care should be taken in preparing the final detailed drawing, particularly with respect to track locations. Use the largest convenient scale, perhaps full size, and accurate templates. Templates are especially important if you are using commercial track products such as turnouts and fixed-radius curved track sections. With hand-laid track or flexible track sections there is more opportunity for adjustment during construction.

8.6 DESIGNING FOR PREFABRICATED TRACK

Two types of prefabricated track have long been available. One consists of flexible track sections 3' (.91m) long, switches, and crossings intended to be spiked down and brought to exact gauge by the modeler. Except for the limited variety available, design for this type of prefabricated track is essentially no different than designing for hand-laid track. However the templates made for design should be based on the commercial products, crossings as well as turnouts. See Section 6.3 for information on the use of templates.

The second type of prefabricated track are the short lengths of tangents and fixed-radius curves designed to be plugged together with similarly-made turnouts and crossings (even double slip switches in N gauge). If a layout is to be designed using such track components exclusively, it is vital that the plans be accurate. Forcing the track to conform to a plan may result in poor matching of the ends of the prefabrication pieces. To assure accuracy the templates

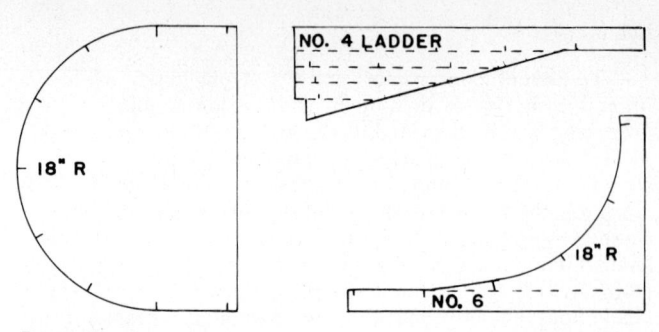

Fig. 10 Templates for sectional track

should not be just for individual pieces but for common combinations with the endings of the individual pieces marked. Fig. 10 shows templates for combinations of track sections.

Books have been available covering specific layout designs made with the commercial products of a particular manufacturer. Some of these books have included diagrams of useful complex trackage giving the specific pieces of sectional track, switches, and crossings necessary to construct that trackage. A diagram of this type appears in Fig. 11.

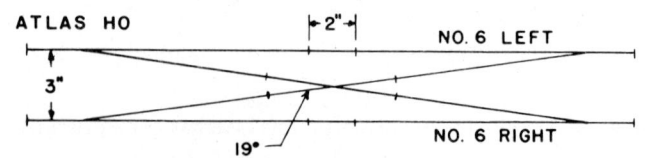

Fig. 11 Prefabricated track scissors crossover

Even if it is desired to use sectional track exclusively, design and construction is simpler if one, perhaps more, pieces of flexible track are included as indicated in Fig. 12. It is then no longer necessary to determine exactly how many and what pieces are required for an exact fit nor must the track be laid with great precision. The piece of flexible track can be cut and bent to the shape needed to make a smooth connection between the sectional-track pieces.

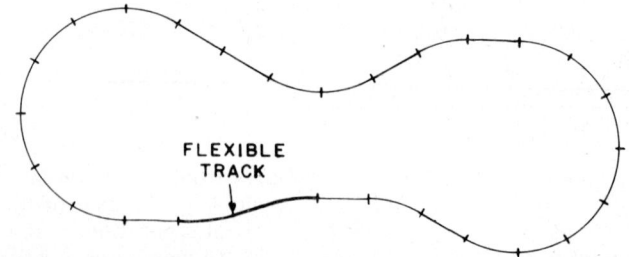

Fig. 12 Adjusting with flexible track

8.7 CLEARANCE AND OVERHANG

Small layouts typically use short radii yet often operate with sizable cars and locomotives. Such equipment has considerable overhang when on the curves. Provision must be made in the form of increased distance between track centers and clearance to trackside obstructions such as girders of a through plate-girder bridge. If bridges with standard clearances are installed, the track approaching the bridge should be straight for one locomotive length (Section 6.9).

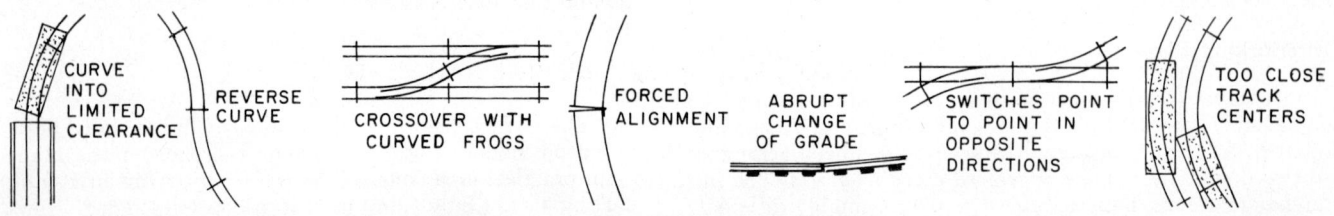

Fig. 13. Errors to avoid when using sectional track.

CHAPTER 9
FINAL DESIGN

9.1 GENERAL

Final or detail design, as defined in this Handbook, determines exact locations and results in the final design drawing used to construct the railroad. Except to check critical points, detailed design should not be undertaken until preliminary design has been completed to the point where all reasonable approaches to the overall plan have been considered.

Actually there are two stages in the detailed planning step. The first creates the final design on paper and is the subject of this Chapter. The second stage is laying out the plans full size on the roadbed. Many of the fine details are placed at this full-size stage, for example the exact drawing of easements. However this second stage is usually considered part of trackwork or scenery construction and is outside the scope of this Handbook. Track construction methods and procedures may be found in the references cited in Section 6.1.

9.2 SCALE OF DRAWING

The scale of the final drawing should be large enough to show all the necessary details including the locations of switch points and frogs. This is in contrast to preliminary drawings which should have a scale small enough that the overall relationship of tracks can easily be visualized. The smallest practical limits of scale for final drawings are about $3/4'' = 1'$, a ratio of 16:1 for HO, double that for N and half for O. The upper limit is usually set by the size of the paper available and large layouts may have to be divided into sections. Some model railroaders, Frank McKenna, MMR, for example, spread out wrapping paper and made the final drawing full size. On a very small layout, say an N scale layout on a 2' by 6' (0.6 by 1.8m) table, full size is probably the most appropriate scale.

Complex trackage requires more exact planning than simple track. It may be advantageous to draw the over-all final plan to a scale which creates a convenient size of drawing but have separate drawings to a larger scale of complex areas.

9.3 SEQUENCE OF DESIGN

The final design starts at critical or important points. For example there may be only one position in which a curve of the minimum radius may be placed. Complex trackage generally should be designed early as such points often determine the exact location of the approaching tracks. If different minimum radii and grades have been adopted for main and branch lines, the main lines should have their final alignments determined first as it is easier to adjust the branches to suit. Spurs and side tracks for industrial areas are usually best left to the last as long as space is reserved for them. Often the number and location of auxiliary tracks and spurs as designed during the detailed phase are considerably different from those sketched in during the preliminary planning, as in the spurs at Whitehouse in Fig. 2. An excellent technique is to sketch side tracks on the plan, then after the main tracks and sidings have been drawn full size on the benchwork, design the industrial and similar tracks full size on the benchwork. Their locations then are transferred to the plans.

Scenic effects and drainage are also important parts of detailed design. Such matters should be of continuing concern for, as the sub-roadbed is installed, it becomes easier and easier to visualize how the terrain will look. In particular attention should be given to breaking up what would otherwise be plain embankments or a succession of steep hills or cliffs from line to line.

Fig. 1 Trestle to eliminate cliff

Fig. 1 shows a 6'9" (2m) long deck plate-girder trestle built over a mirror which was added to the plans during detailed planning to eliminate a steep slope and cliff from the upper to the lower tracks. Adding the trestle opened up an apparent cross valley which created space for a small town and industrial tracks. Fig. 18, Chapter 4 is a photograph of a 5'10" (1.8m) long concrete-arch trestle also built over a mirror. This trestle was added after the track was laid to break up a long, essentially uniform slope. In short, design

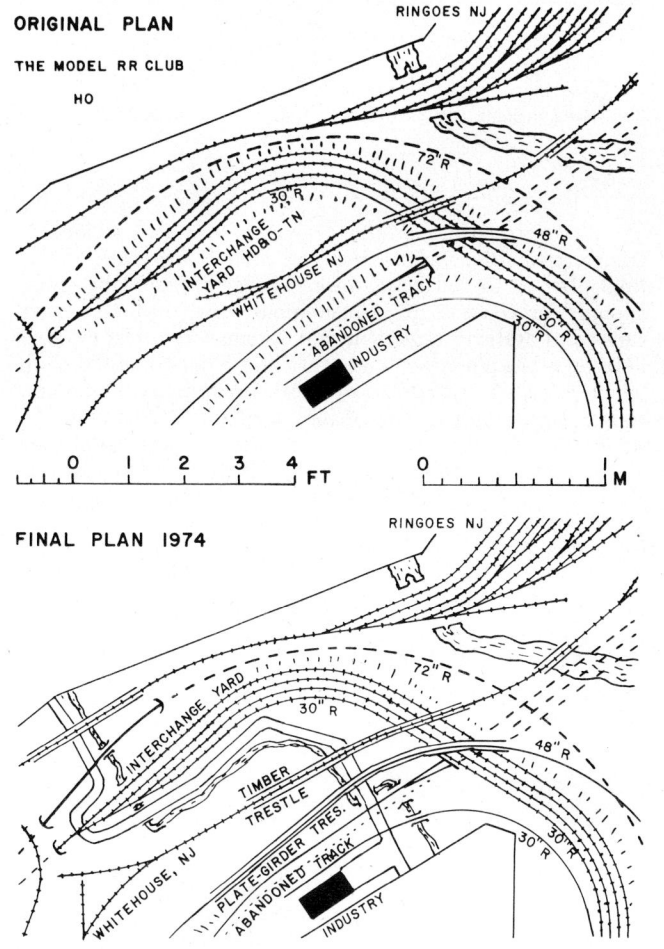

Fig. 2 Preliminary to final design

does not stop when tracks start to go down.

Fig. 2 is another example of continuous detail planning. The preliminary plan at the top shows a watershed leading to a sizable stream on the right. After several of the sub-roadbeds had been placed, it became apparent that there were too many near-vertical rises between tracks. These are indicated by the hachures. Therefore a valley was planned as shown at the bottom of the figure. This modification eliminated most of the steep slopes, reduced those which remained, opened up operator visibility to the interchange yard, and broke up the ridge extending down the middle of the benchwork. Note the small stream at the bottom of this added valley and the culverts. Always provide for drainage. It is an important detail often missing on models.

9.4 FINAL DRAWING

For larger layouts, it is important that the final design produce a master plan which can be up-dated as the railroad grows. This master plan should be a tracing to permit its duplication by any standard process for all work should be done using copies, not the master itself.

One time-proven method of making a master is to draw the plan in pencil on drafting film rather than drafting paper for greater durability. As the track is laid and structures installed, their actual locations are carefully measured and drawn in ink on the master plan. This method clearly indicates on the copies which tracks have not yet been built and therefore a more readily subject to change.

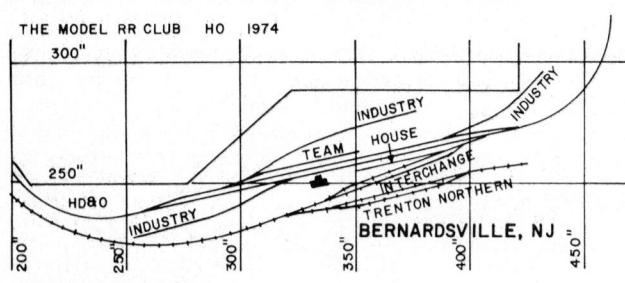

Fig. 3 Grid on plans

9.5 GRID

Accurate grids on the drawings are convenient for transferring information from the preliminary plan to the final plan or to the benchwork. The grid should be small enough for convenient measurements with ordinary steel tapes and drafting scales but not so small that the number of lines on the plans becomes confusing. The Model RR Club which used a computer to draw its preliminary plans and thus could easily try various grids, tested 1' (30.5 cm), 50" (127cm), and 100" (245cm) grids. The 50" size combined with engineers scales rather than architects scales proved the best of the three. If possible, a distinctive color for the grid is helpful.

After the benchwork was constructed, the tops of all its members were painted white and, using a chalk line, an accurate grid corresponding to the 50" grid on the drawings was marked on every member a grid line crossed. A zero elevation datum level was also marked at many points on the benchwork. By measuring from the grid and from the zero elevation, risers would be installed and sub-roadbed placed at any point with complete confidence it was correct without waiting for nearby sub-roadbed to be installed. Fig. 3 shows one of the stations and the grid.

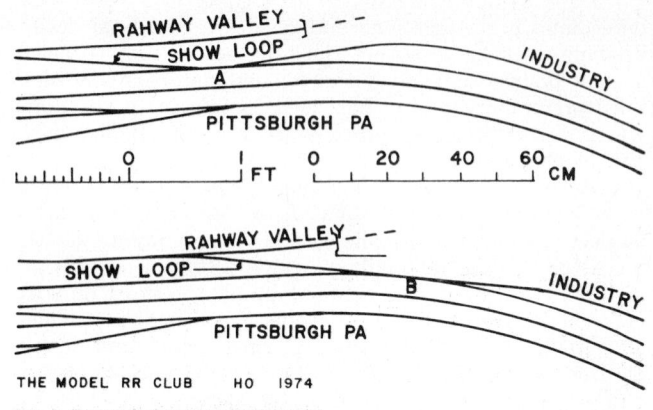

Fig. 4 Detailed design improvement

9.6 DETAILED CHECKING FOR STANDARDS

Although all design standards should be observed when making preliminary plans, the small scale of such drawings combined with the emphasis placed on the overall railroad and the simple sketching-in of industrial tracks and the like usually introduce minor violations of standards which are overlooked. If, as recommended in this Handbook, the preliminary design does not stretch the design rules to their limit, minor changes to rectify such violations are easily accomplished either on the final drawing or full size on the roadbed. Fig. 4 is an example of a change actually made during the final design of the yard shown in Fig. 7 of Chapter 7. At A is the show loop connection and a turnout to an industrial spur to the same scale as the preliminary plan drawn. A detailed look showed a reverse curve for trains using the show loop and the track, as built, was changed to that shown at B.

Reverse curves and insufficient clearances are two of the most likely violations of standards which can be carried over from preliminary plans. Particularly if tight-radius curves are used, it is necessary to check that adequate clearance has been left for the overhang of steam locomotives and long cars. For example a tight radius curve cannot be led directly up to a through bridge of standard widths. (Section 6.9).

The time required for checking every point on the layout before track is laid is well spent.

Chapter 10
PASSENGER FACILITIES

10.1 GENERAL

In contrast with most prototype railroads, passenger operation is included on the great majority of model lines. Model passenger trains and their facilities such as terminals and coach yards are not only interesting in their own right but also increase operational opportunities through the need to mesh freight and passenger trains.

This Chapter covers not only passenger-only facilities such as Pullman service tracks but also combined freight and passenger stations. Such combined stations save space and thus are the most suitable station for the smallest layouts and are useful for secondary stations on even the largest of layouts.

For further information on passenger service see 'Passenger Terminals and Trains' by John A. Droege republished by Kalmbach Publishing Co., Milwaukee, Wis.

10.2 PASSENGER STATIONS

Through Stations

Through stations, also called side stations, have continuous primary tracks so arriving trains may continue without reverse movement. The great majority of prototype stations are of this type.

The simplest station is a short platform with pedestrian access. Such stations are often flag stops (stop on signal) but may be scheduled stops. The Mine Brook station on the DL&W was a short platform extending from a road grade crossing alongside a single track. It once had a roofed, open-sided shelter. In 1957 it was a scheduled stop for two trains and a flag stop for nine others. Such platform-only stations existed on multi-track lines as well. On a model they are a space-saving way of justifying station stops.

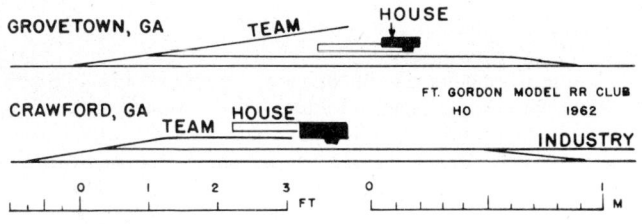

Fig. 1 Combination station

When a small passenger station includes a station building more substantial than a shelter, often a combination freight and passenger station was constructed. This compact arrangement is well suited to models and Fig. 1 shows two examples taken from an actual layout. The top station is a model of the station of the same name on the Georgia RR. The side track was the house track, not a siding.

The passenger and freight stations may be separate even at small stations (Fig. 1, Chapter 11). The passenger station then may be placed at its most advantageous position. On the prototype this is usually the side on which the greater number of passengers board. Particularly on a commuter line, a substantial passenger station may be placed alongside main tracks remote from any side track or siding.

If a siding exists, it is common practice to locate the passenger station opposite the siding so meets or passings are possible during station stops. There are, however, prototype and model examples where the passenger station is on the main track beyond the siding either to place the station more convenient to the town or to free the switching tracks from the interference of a train making a station stop. Fig. 2 is an example on a model where space for the station existed only at the end of the siding. Fig. 18, Chapter 4, is a photograph of the trestle indicated in Fig. 2.

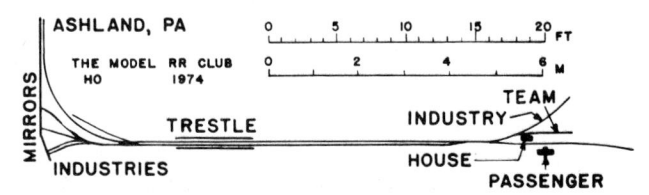

Fig. 2 Station at end of siding

Although sidings at stations usually are long enough for most if not all passenger trains, the platforms may be short, sometimes just one car length. At more important stations platforms tend to be close to the length of trains. Nevertheless, even at some of the largest prototype stations, the longest trains exceeded the platform length. At Newark, N.J. passengers for the last two Pullmans on the Penn-Texas had to walk through the train. This same train made two station stops at the Columbus, Ohio Union Station: one stop for the head end through the first Pullman, and a second stop for the rear Pullmans. At St. Louis the Texas Eagle (MOP) was divided and backed into two platform tracks.

Passenger platforms need not block access to a side track. There are numerous examples of tracks crossing platforms. At Fayetteville, N.C. on the ACL a spur was led through a platform. Even the busy La Salle St. terminal in Chicago, once used by the 20th Century Limited, had ladder tracks crossing the platforms.

Platforms are not necessarily installed for every track. Murray Hill, N.J. (Fig. 1, Chapter 11), had a platform only on the main track. Non-platform tracks can be used for through movements, many examples existed on the PRR four-track lines where platforms were often built only for the two outside tracks.

At a few stations on the CRRNJ four-track main, platforms for the two outside tracks were extended by pavement between the rails to make platforms for the two center tracks. Fig. 3 is a model of one of these four-track stations.

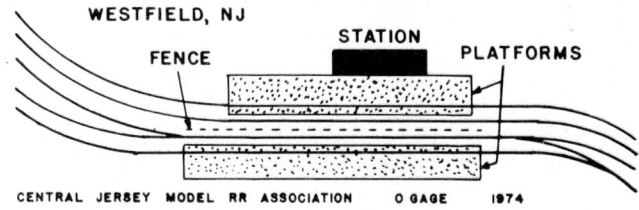

Fig. 3 Four-track station

When passenger service is featured, even a small layout can have more than one station. Fig. 4 shows a portable layout with three stations as designed by Henry T. Wilhelm and built by the NYSME. This layout suffered from being built in two pieces with many tracks crossing between the halves.

Since extra tracks are useful at junctions, it saves space on a model to place the large through stations at

Chapter 10   47

junctions. Many prototype examples existed, among them Back Bay in Boston and Englewood in Chicago. Fig. 2, Chapter 13 gives a prototype example which has been modeled twice.

Some through stations also serve terminating traffic. The prototype often installed stub tracks at such stations in addition to the through tracks, the P&LE and PRR stations in Pittsburgh were two examples. Even small stations where cars were dropped might have stub tracks. Banff on the CP had several such tracks for the cars bringing visitors to the park. On a model, stub tracks have the advantage of saving space. (Fig. 7, Chapter 7 and Fig. 9, Chapter 11).

Another space-saving prototype is a two-level station where the upper tracks are over the lower. In Philadelphia there were two examples on the PRR. The main 30th St. station had suburban platforms crossing over the main-line platforms and a two-track suburban station had one track over the other with platforms on both. Sometimes different types of rail lines were on the different levels. At Oakland, Cal. interurban platforms were above the SP station. In Newark, N.J. a three-level station still existed in 1976 with rapid transit on the top level, RR and rapid transit on the middle, and PCC cars on the lowest level.

10.3 HEAD STATIONS

Head, also called stub, stations have their main tracks terminating at bumping posts or reversing loops. On the prototype, as well as on the model, the majority of the largest passenger stations are of this type. Some stations classified as head stations such as Washington, D.C. also had through tracks.

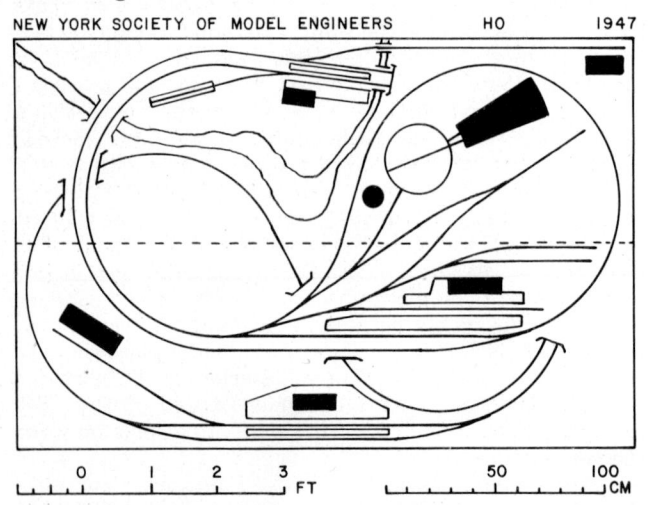

Fig. 4 Portable layout featuring passenger service

Not all head stations are large. Stations at the end of branches or small railroads sometimes had but a single track, Fig. 6 gives some prototype examples.

Terminal stations sometimes are built on the line side of the terminal yard, an example being Bay Head Junction on the NY&LB. These are through stations. On the model, due to the greater level of activity in comparison with most prototype stations, there is great advantage in using a head

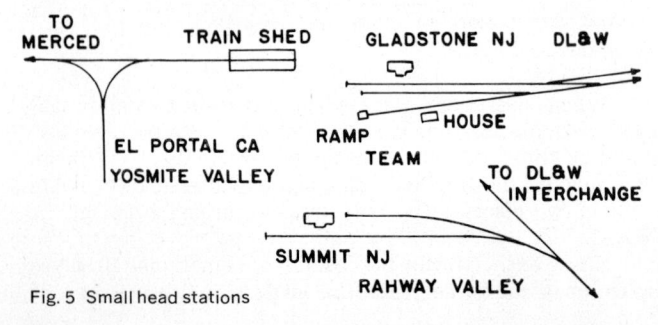

Fig. 5 Small head stations

station as passenger trains are then out of the way of switching activities while they are standing in the station.

For a model of a large station, head stations are more suited to the limitations imposed by benchwork than are through stations. Fig. 6 shows four different locations for head stations. Even small layouts can have a sizable head station if arranged as at A. See also Fig. 4, Chapter 8. Benchwork peninsulas are excellent sites for head stations as at B. See Fig. 24 of Chapter 7 for three head stations on peninsulas on a single medium-size layout.

Corners of benchwork as at C can be used for head stations but not for through stations. To give the illusion of a large through station, a head station can be built against a mirror as at D. A station concourse against the mirror and over the tracks as indicated helps create the desired effect.

Modelers tend to place an 'escape' crossover near the ends of stub tracks at stations in the expectation that road locomotives will uncouple and go directly to the engine house without waiting for a switcher to pull the train away. Such cross overs were rare on the prototype and where provided were seldom used except at small stations where the locomotive uncoupled, ran around the train, and coupled for the return trip. The general prototype practice is to uncouple the road locomotive then, after the train is unloaded, to remove the cars with a switcher. Only then does the road locomotive leave. At some head stations the trains were backed into the platform tracks: New Orleans, St. Louis, and El Portal on the Yosemite Valley were just some of the examples. It is difficult to consider escape crossovers anything other than a waste of switch machines at terminals with switchers.

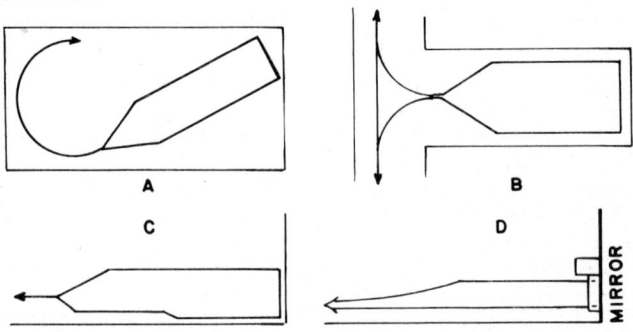

Fig. 6 Locations for large head stations

10.4 WATERFRONT TERMINALS

From a modeler's point of view the chief difference between a waterfront terminal and a conventional station is its scenic surroundings. The combination of rail and water facilities make an interesting model and, if there is more than one station, provides contrast.

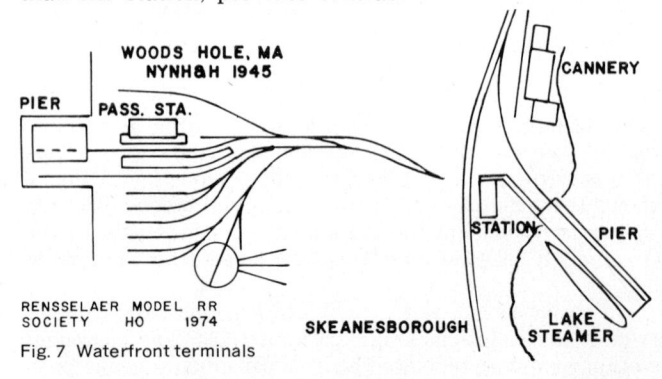

Fig. 7 Waterfront terminals

Many waterfront head stations had their bumping posts at a concourse leading directly to the ferry slips or perhaps through a station to the slips. New York harbor, Camden, N.J., and Oakland, Cal. had large examples. Models of the Hoboken terminal appear in Fig. 11. On the left of Fig. 7 is smaller head station at Woods Hole, MA. Even

Chapter 10

narrow-gauge lines had waterfront terminals, specifically the Northwestern Pacific (Sausalito, CA) and the Boston, Revere Beach and Lynn.

There were also examples of through stations where cars were dropped and placed shipside as on the CP at Ft. William, Ontario. A model example of such a terminal is on the right in Fig. 7.

A special case of waterfront terminals were those where some of the cars or perhaps complete trains were loaded on car ferries.

10.5 STATION DESIGN

Small passenger stations with one or two platform tracks present no design problems other than finding the necessary space for the building and the operating problems caused by passenger trains making a station stop. Combination stations, Fig. 1, do require a house track but, again as such stations are small, this also is mostly a matter of finding the space.

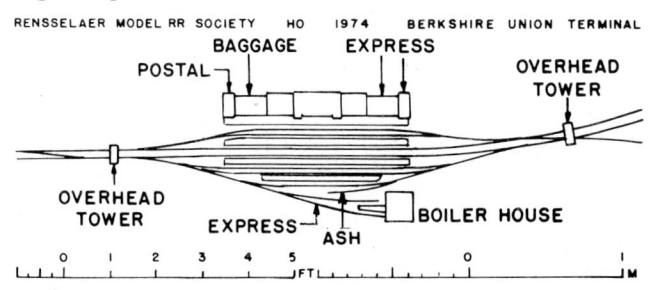

Fig. 8 Passenger station

Multi-track stations or stations where trains are worked by adding or removing cars require more careful planning. Perhaps the most common single fault of large model passenger terminals is inadequate approach tracks (throats). It is important to think through the various moves which will be required. For example can a switcher bring up a diner and cut it into the train without blocking critical tracks? See Section 10.6 for the design of throats.

The station building or buildings are a matter of structures and scenery. The layout design must, however, provide the necessary space for such facilities as a baggage room, express, main, and a waiting room. Fig. 8 shows a model of the Troy, N.Y. Union Station.

Access to platform tracks may be simple, just walking across the intervening tracks as in Fig. 3 or at Williams Junction on the Santa Fe. At the latter station passengers sometimes had to climb through the Grand Canyon Limited to reach the Super Chief.

Under-track passageways for passengers and, often, another for baggage and mail trucks, were widely used and are easy to model. They are included in the model stations of Figs. 3 and 8. Placing much of the station under the tracks is a space-saving method which has several prototypes including the 1950 NYC station in Syracuse, N.Y.

Overhead passageways to the platforms were most often used when the station waiting rooms were above track level. If the overhead concourse is the main waiting room as was the case at several large prototype stations including the Union Station, Columbus, Ohio and even some small ones as the Peachtree Station on the Southern in Atlanta, space can be saved over placing the station alongside the tracks as in Fig. 8.

Fig. 9 shows the minimum width of platforms between tracks based on prototype practice. Since a model station is not concerned with passenger and baggage truck movements, it is possible to go below the minimums shown with no disadvantage except in terms of realistic appearance. For simplicity many modelers double the normal track spacings at platforms. Customarily platforms extend into the beginning of the throat although this means widths below those shown in Fig. 9.

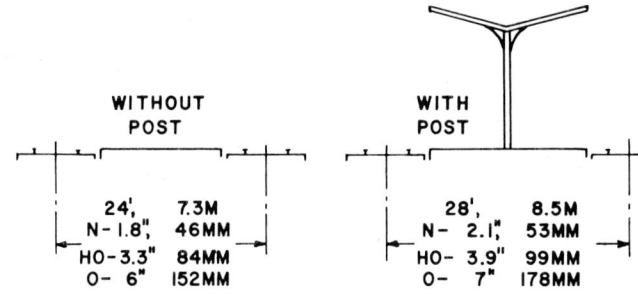

Fig. 9 Minimum platform widths

Platform protection which completely covers the tracks such as the old arched train shed still existing (1974) at Reading Terminal, Philadelphia, the smaller, modern flat-roofed shed at Milwaukee, or continuous roofs supported on posts such as at Penn-Central Station, Pittsburgh, block access and visibility to the tracks. Unless some specific prototype is being modeled, it is better to choose the butterfly shelter as in Fig. 9 or the older umbrella platform shelter as these do not cover the tracks.

10.6 THROATS

The tracks approaching the platforms of a station are called the throat and are critical in determining how much traffic the station can handle. Since passenger traffic is usually more dense on a model than on the prototype, throat design, if anything, is more critical on the model.

Through stations have two throats, head stations but one. In addition trains can be worked from both ends at a through station. Therefore, for the same number of trains, the throat for a head station must be capable of handling twice the traffic as each throat of a through station plus having additional features to permit switchers to operate effectively from just one end.

As a general rule a throat should begin as far from the platform tracks as space permits. In particular, freight trains should be diverted from the platform tracks early. Fig. 7, Chapter 7 shows a model terminal where a single-track line divides into a freight and a passenger main track .9 scale miles (1.5 scale km) before the platforms. Parallel tracks should be provided to permit a switcher to bring cars to and from the coach yard and express tracks without blocking trains.

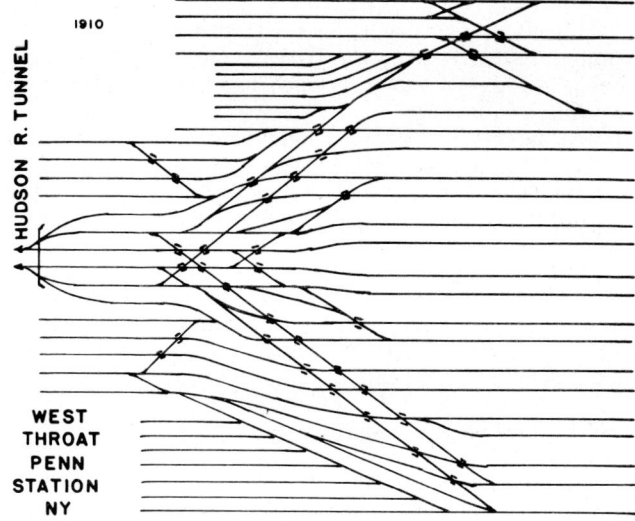

Fig. 10 Prototype throat

Although the station itself is too large to model, Pennsylvania Station, N.Y. was designed for a limited space, only about 1,300' (400m) from the portal of the double-track Hudson River tunnel to the platforms. This is only 15' (4.6m) in HO yet great flexibility has been provided.

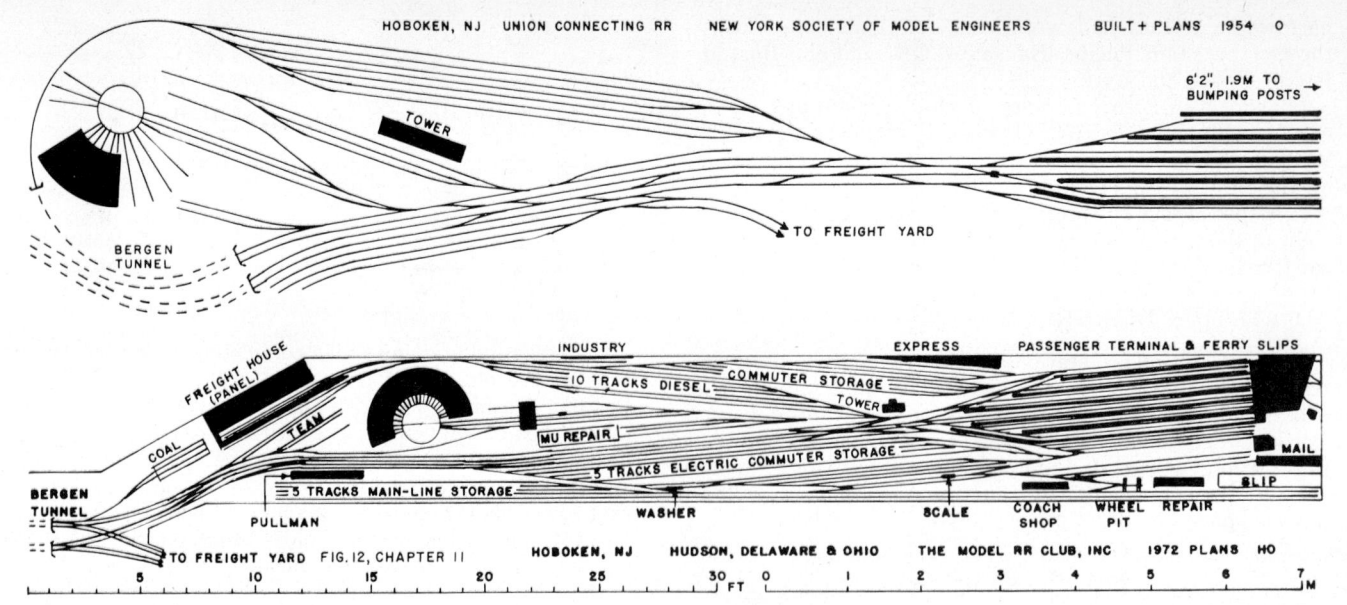

Fig. 11 Large model passenger terminals

This throat is shown in diagram form in Fig. 10. Part of the double Y throat at St. Louis is shown in Fig. 12.

Model stations seldom approximate the size of the largest prototype stations but Fig. 11 shows two model examples based on the same prototype, Hoboken Terminal on the DL&W. The O scale terminal was being built by the New York Society of Model Engineers when they were located in the terminal building itself. The HO version is part of the design for expansion shown in Fig. 23, Chapter 7. In both cases crossovers at the west end of the Bergen Tunnel serve as part of the throat. These terminals were designed to duplicate the frequent commuter service of the prototype.

10.7 PASSENGER YARDS

The common prototype practice was to place passenger yards where they would be easily accessible from the throat. Even where space was limited, such as at Grand Central in N.Y., a small coach yard was often placed at the station but in such cases the main yards were some distance away, Mott Haven in the Bronx in the case of Grand Central. The yards at Penn Station, N.Y. can be seen in Fig. 10. Even a small head station may require a sizable coach yard. The station at Gladstone on the DL&W, Fig. 5, had the yard shown in Fig. 6, Chapter 5 which has been duplicated on two different layouts.

At larger stations passenger yards may be divided by class of equipment. Fig. 11 shows MU, diesel commuter, and main-line storage based on the actual prototype of the station. In the terminal of Fig. 7, Chapter 7 there is a special Pullman servicing track.

The St. Louis terminal had separate yards for coaches and for head-end cars as can be seen in Fig. 12. However at the Waldo Yard, Jersey City on the PRR (used before Penn Station opened, capacity 320 cars) there was no separation of Pullmans or dining cars from the coaches.

10.8 EXPRESS AND MAIL

At small stations express and mail were handled directly on the passenger platforms while trains made station stops. This was also true at large stations for the limited trains. Nevertheless even small stations might have a separate room for handling express.

Larger stations often had express and mail cars dropped there. If such stations had an overhead or underground passageway to platform tracks, the track next to the station building might be reserved for express and mail. Other stations provided a special track near the station for the purpose (Fig. 8).

Terminals often had major express facilities with multi-track platforms. These facilities might be part of the station building or a separate building immediately adjacent to the passenger station. South Station, Boston was an example of the latter. More often the express terminal was more remote but still served by the same throat as in Washington, D.C. In Chicago an express terminal building near the Union Station was built over the express platform tracks, a

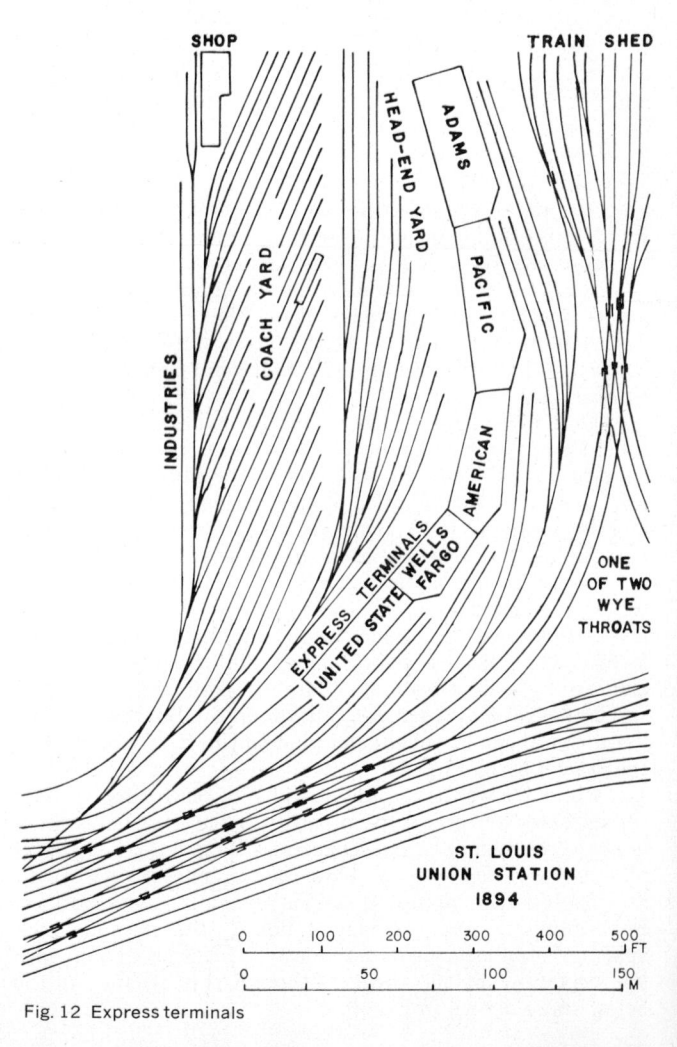

Fig. 12 Express terminals

Chapter 10

space-saving prototype which was followed in the model terminal of Fig. 7, Chapter 7.

By 1974 many of the express facilities were abandoned or removed. In the immediate past most were for Railway Express but at stations built around the turn of the century there usually were facilities for several express companies. Fig. 12 shows how a building with an interesting shape was fitted against one of the wye throats at the St. Louis Union Station to house five express companies. Although this terminal is too large to model, it illustrates that the prototype, like the modeler, designs its structures to fit the available space.

Where possible, tracks for mail cars led directly into a government postal building, an example being in Pittsburgh. At Pennsylvania Station, N.Y. mail was handled on platforms in the station separate from the passenger platforms. This was true at several major stations but often the mail cars shared the tracks with the express cars. Some terminals provided a special building for the mail-car track, a model example appearing in Fig. 11.

10.9 CAR SERVICE

Pullman

Terminals with Pullman service often had a Pullman Co. building adjacent to the tracks on which such cars were stored. Model examples can be seen in Fig. 11 and in Fig. 7, Chapter 7.

Coach

Larger stations, particularly terminals, often were equipped with car repair facilities, sometimes a special building for coach repair and another for trucks including a wheel pit at the latter. A model example appears in Fig. 11 and one on the prototype in Fig. 12. Such shops should have separate tracks rather than using one in the coach storage yard. Repair tracks can be short.

MU

MU cars are restricted to that part of the line equipped with overhead or third rail. A shop for such cars often is located at one of the electrified stations, see Fig. 11.

Car Washing

Although working washers are not practical on a model, such facilities are an excellent operating addition to a passenger station. It could be required that all main-line trains go through the washer before being placed on a platform track. There were prototype examples of passenger trains being washed at a point on their run, an example being the California Zephyr at Denver.

Prior to about 1930 car washing was by hand and even in the early seventies the North Coast Limited was hand washed during its station stops at Livingston, Montana. By 1974 most washing was by mechanical washers. As a general rule, washers were placed where a train could pass completely through the machine and continue without returning through the washer, see Fig. 11. However the washer at South Bend on the South Shore was on a stub track in the small terminal yard.

Clint Grant shot this view of Bill McClanahan's passenger station at Purgatory on the Texas & Rio Grande Western. Passenger terminal is 11 tracks wide. Old Victorian station was built from John P. Allen plans in Railroad Model Craftsman. A passenger facility this large on a private model railroad is unusual and very delightful.

Chapter 11
FREIGHT FACILITIES

11.1 GENERAL

Freight movements based on the prototype are regarded by many as the most interesting part of model operation. In contrast with passenger service where cars have limited moves and train consists remain essentially constant, each freight car can have a separate point of origin and a different destination from all other cars. The key to interesting freight operation is to give each car a definite purpose. A loaded car is sent to a consignee. Empty cars may be sent to shippers, returned through interchange to their owning road, or concentrated by the car distributor in the area where they will be needed.

The possibilities of freight operation cannot be exploited, however, unless the necessary freight facilities are included in the design of the layout. The number and type of facilities must be in accordance with the concept and within the limitations of the space available. Even the smallest layouts can have tracks which serve as points of origin and as destination for cars. Tracks must be provided to receive trains and for classification. Finally, if space allows, various en-route service facilities can be added such as icing platforms. This Chapter covers the various tracks and facilities required for interesting freight operation from simple industrial spurs to hump yards suitable for layouts ranging from the smallest to the largest so far built. Prototype examples too large to be modeled are outside the scope of this Handbook.

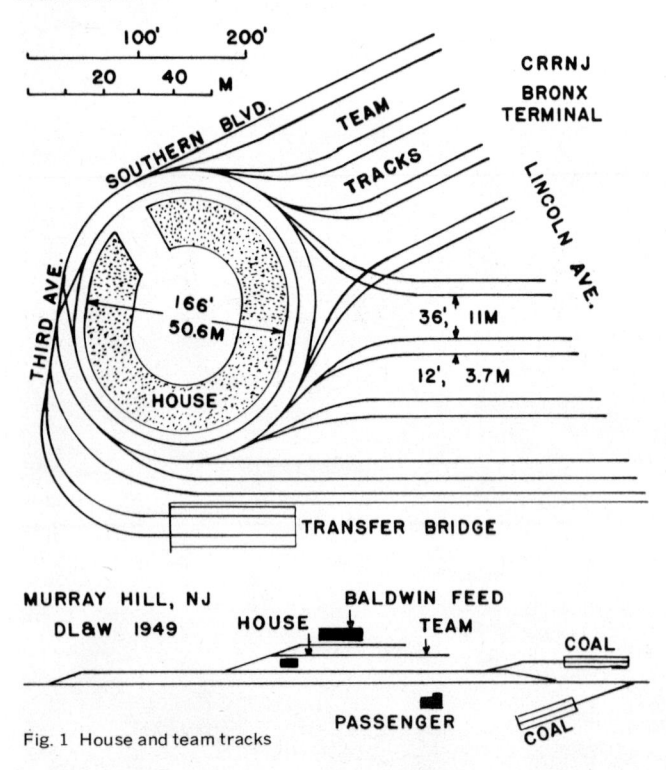

Fig. 1 House and team tracks

11.2 CAR DESTINATIONS

If a freight car is to be moved in a prototype-like manner, that move must be to reach a preselected destination. As used in this Handbook, destination means any point to which a car is sent. Obviously each destination serves as the origination point for the next move.

On large and medium-size layouts, a wide variety of destinations can and should be provided to justify many types of cars. When space is limited, there is advantage in selecting those types of destinations, such as team tracks and interchange, which handle a variety of cars rather than tracks essentially special for one class of traffic, e.g., a coal pocket.

Team and House Tracks

Team and freight-house tracks are public facilities for those without private side tracks. Freight houses are for LCL (Less than Car Load) and are serviced primarily by box cars. Team tracks are for loading directly to or from wagons or trucks and are particularly useful on models as logical destinations for almost every type of car except those requiring special facilities.

When a layout is large enough for two or more stations, there is merit in having a house and team track at each. Thus two destinations are available which do not require special records or instructions on a station basis.

At small stations the house and team tracks may be different locations on the same track. A prototype example is given at the bottom of Fig. 1. Large cities usually had multi-track team yards and multi-platform freight houses. Such facilities might be adjacent or widely separated. Fig. 1 shows the Bronx Terminal of the CRRNJ which was exclusively house and team tracks. It was a complete railroad which could be modeled in HO on a table 5.5' by 7' (1.7 by 2.1m).

In general a house track was adjacent to a freight platform but it was not rare for an additional house track to be placed with its cars serviced by crossing through the cars on the platform tracks. This is a space-saving technique of increasing the car capacity of a freight house.

Produce terminals

A produce terminal provides an excellent destination for refrigerator cars and special cars such as those for watermelons. A produce terminal usually is a combination of a specialized team yard for unloading directly into refrigerator trucks and of a refrigerated warehouse serving the same function as the freight house excepting being only for produce.

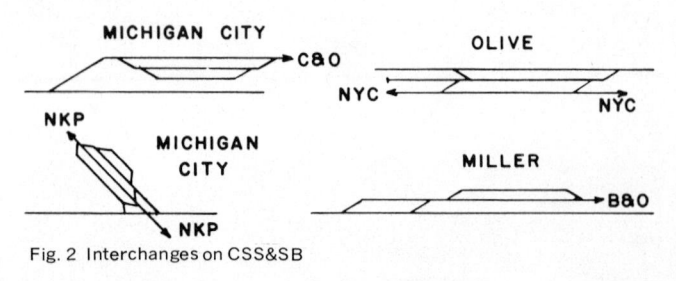

Fig. 2 Interchanges on CSS&SB

Foreign Interchange

Foreign interchange, i.e., to a different railroad, is the most powerful generator of traffic which can be included on a model railroad. Interchange can handle all types of cars and in any numbers. Fig. 2 shows four of the interchanges on the South Shore. All are of modelable size. Fig. 6, Chapter 2 shows the two interchanges on the Hoboken shore, a prototype switching line. One is an interchange yard with connecting railroads, the other a transfer bridge to car floats. Two interchange points justify much traffic between them.

On a model, when space permits two separate lines, actual interchange between the two lines offers great possibilities. Fig. 13, Chapter 4 shows a three-way interchange among a railroad, an interurban, and a switching line with a separate four-track interchange yard for the interurban. In Fig. 6, Chapter 5, the interchange between the interurban and the railroad uses tracks in the railroad yard. Another model interchange is shown in Fig. 3, Chapter 9.

Even if a complete separate line cannot be included, enough of a foreign line can be built to remove cars sent to interchange. In Fig. 10, Chapter 2 a B&O reversing loop received interchange from a terminal and returned it later to the same terminal. Also a short stretch of the Reading RR accepted interchange from one point and returned it to another station. Fig. 3 shows an interchange possibility based on the actual operation of the Scioto Valley, an interurban line in Ohio. Traction motors pick up loaded coal hoppers from the C&O interchange and deliver them to the power plant and return with empty hoppers. The C&O exists only to bring the loaded hoppers back to interchange and return the empties to the power plant.

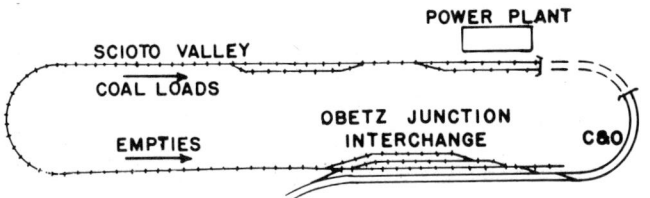

Fig. 3 Interchange for return of cars

Storage Tracks

Unless there is some specific need, such as preparing for a grain movement, prototype railroads do not store cars of foreign railroads. They return them as soon as possible to avoid per-diem charges. Model railroads could, but seldom if ever, simulate the return of foreign cars by physically removing them from the layout at an interchange point. Instead all freight cars on a model railroad are customarily treated alike whether lettered for the home road or not. So, on a model, storage is a usual destination for all types of cars.

The prototype may provide storage tracks at major yards, but usually only for holding cars temporarily. The BN Balmer Yard, Seattle had seven stub storage tracks. Model storage yards can be seen in Figs. 9 and 12. For permanent storage common prototype practices are to use side tracks alongside the main, remote from congested areas or yards no longer in active operating service.

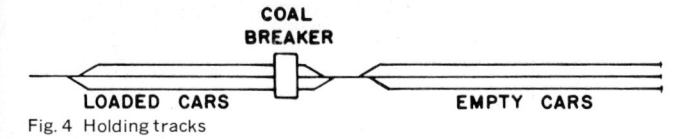

Fig. 4 Holding tracks

Holding Tracks

When the destination itself cannot receive all the cars directed there, for example empty hoppers for a mine or loaded hoppers to a coal dumper, holding tracks are provided. Fig. 4 shows empty and loaded holding tracks at a coal mine. Incoming empties are pushed through into the stub holding tracks. As empties are needed they are moved from the empty holding tracks through the breaker and, after loading, onto the loaded holding tracks. On the prototype these movements may be by gravity or winch but on a model a small locomotive stationed at the breaker is more practical. See Section 11.4 for the problems of gravity operation on a model.

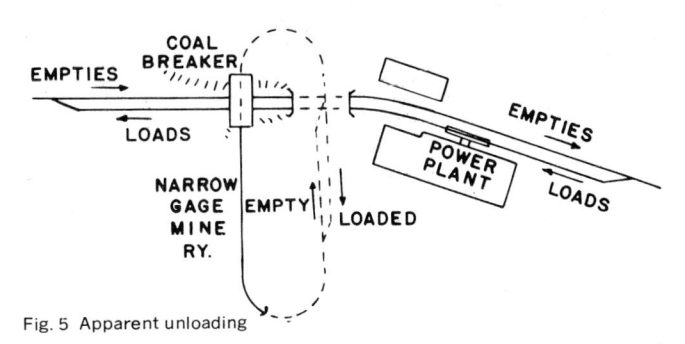

Fig. 5 Apparent unloading

Holding tracks for complementary destinations can be made continuous, an example being given in Fig. 5. Loaded hoppers delivered to the power plant appear from under the coal breaker as though being moved by a car puller and empty hoppers delivered to the mine appear at the power plant. Although the two destinations must be separated scenically, they should be physically close so the number of cars between the two will not be great. This same principle was used with an interchange in Fig. 3.

Also shown in Fig. 5 is a narrow-gauge mine railway on which two identical trains circulate in opposite directions, one loaded and one empty.

In Fig. 12 holding tracks can be seen for a coal unloader and a transfer bridge on a model.

Fig. 6 TOFC facilities

TOFC

TOFC (Trailer On Flat Car) service requires tracks with loading and unloading facilities. This may be a simple ramp at the end of a spur as on the left in Fig. 6. Sometimes a flat car with one truck removed serves as the ramp. For end-ramp unloading the trailers must face the ramps so turning tracks are needed.

Large TOFC facilities may have a crane, center of Fig. 6, or off-track lifting equipment as on the right to remove or load trailers from the side. These two methods require more space than most modelers are willing to devote to TOFC. End-ramp spurs are widely used (Figs. 9, 10, 12 and also Fig. 22, Chapter 7 and Fig. 13, Chapter 4). An end ramp on a team track would allow that track to serve TOFC also.

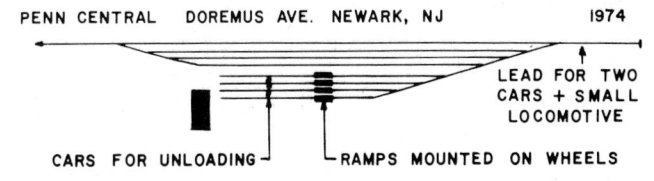

Fig. 7 Autorack terminal

Autorack

Prototype railroads maintain public facilities for unloading automobiles from autorack cars. These may be similar to the end-ramp TOFC tracks except the ramp must be adjustable to unload from three levels. To avoid damage to the automobiles, the railroads prefer not to drive the automobiles through several cars to unload. A small locomotive is stationed at the terminal shown in Fig. 7 to spot cuts of not more than two cars at the unloading positions. Trailer-mounted ramps are then positioned at the ends of the cuts.

Chapter 11   53

Container Terminals

Containers of many types have been used by the railroads and interurbans over the years. In the thirties the PRR had an extensive LCL container service, the NYC bulk containers. Usually special container terminals were built at key points for such service, the equipment depending on the containers to be handled.

In-Transit Destinations

Although the waybill takes the car to an ultimate destination, there are intermediate destinations which can add operational interest. Non-mechanical refrigerator cars must be iced and mechanical refrigerators fueled. If an icing platform with fueling facilities is added (Fig. 7, Chapter 7), all refrigerator cars passing through the station can be required to be spotted at the icing platform for a specified time. The same applies to livestock cars as the law requires most stock to be taken from the cars for a rest at specified intervals. Many loaded cars must be weighed before they leave the originating carrier. This requires a track scale. Examples of in-transit destinations can be seen in Figs. 9, 10 and 12. See also Section 11.4.

Industrial Tracks

In this Handbook the term industrial track means a track serving an industry or commercial enterprise of any sort as distinguished from public facilities such as team tracks or tracks used by the railroad itself.

As a general rule many small industrial tracks create more operational interest than a few large ones. The small prototype station of Fig. 1 has five destinations—the feed store, two coal pockets, the house track, and the team track. Yet after this station was built to full scale size on the first layout of The Model RR Club, an extra industrial spur was added later and on its second layout the same station was designed with two extra industrial spurs. Experience has shown that, when it is the only responsibility of an operator, a minimum of six destinations is desirable for a station without some other feature such as a junction in order to keep interest high.

The prototype often serves two or more industries with a single track. On a model this added operating interest in the form of removing and replacing cars which block spotting a car further down the spur. Fig. 8 gives examples of multi-industry tracks.

Another method of gaining many destinations in a limited area is to create an industrial district. Because such districts often had tight radii and complex trackage, they make interesting models. Fig. 13, Chapter 4 shows an example. Track standards for industrial tracks should be less restrictive than yards and branch lines to increase the contrast between industrial tracks and the rest of the layout.

11.3 FREIGHT YARDS

11.31 General

Unless only complete trains are run, there must be at least one location where a train can be worked. On the smallest layouts a simple run-around track such as a double-ended siding may be all that can be included (Fig. 1, Chapter 4). The E-L often used the Murray Hill siding, Fig. 1, to place cars ahead of the locomotive and behind the caboose for spotting them in spurs west of Murray Hill and east of the next siding. However, on all but the smallest layouts, it is both interesting and convenient to have at least one yard for switching the cars. Yard, as used on the prototype, can mean a set of tracks for a single purpose, e.g., classification yard or receiving yard, or a yard can be a collection of special purpose yards.

Careful consideration should be given to the various yard functions. Because large yards separate the functions more clearly than do small yards, examples are given of some of the largest yards ever designed for model railroads. Even the largest of model yards is small compared to large prototype yards.

The smaller the yard, the more likely a single track will serve more than one function. Even when separate tracks have been provided, on the prototype as well as on the model, all tracks will be used in the most convenient way. For example a train might depart from a classification track. Nevertheless good design will assure that all the necessary movements are convenient and thus, customarily, tracks will be employed in their designed manner.

11.32 Receiving Tracks

An incoming train enters a receiving track which, if possible, should be a train-length long. A train can be doubled into parallel receiving tracks or, as at Trout Lake, Michigan on the SOO, the rear cars can be left standing on the main track clear of the yard while the front end of the train is being worked.

Fig. 8 Multi-industry tracks

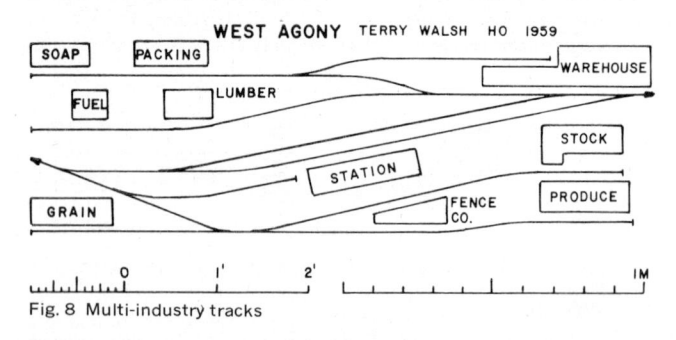

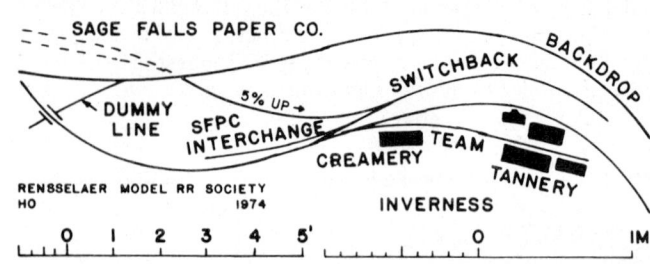

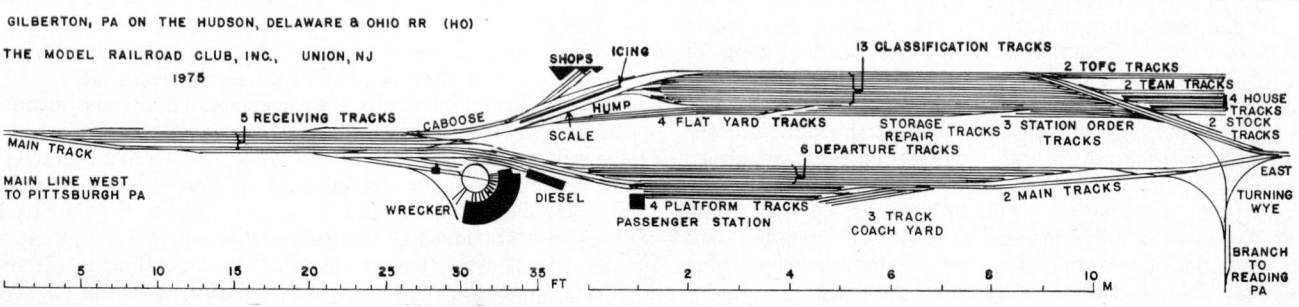

Fig. 9 Model division point with separate yards for major functions

At small yards with infrequent trains, the main track or perhaps the siding might serve as the receiving track. This is always true at small stations which have only those tracks plus some spurs. However model railroads typically have frequent trains so receiving tracks which permit the main and siding to be cleared are very common. A third track paralleling the main track and siding may be sufficient (Fig. 13, Chapter 4).

Where there are several receiving tracks they are called a receiving yard. Large prototype yards often have separate receiving yards for each direction but this is difficult to justify on a model. Fig. 9 shows a large model yard under construction in 1974 which has a clearly identified receiving yard. Eastbound freights enter the receiving yard directly. Westbound freights enter either directly from a main track or, if that route is blocked by a hump move, via the thoroughfare. Two tracks of the receiving yard are continued through the departure yard to handle exceptionally long trains.

When receiving tracks are longer than many of the trains, crossovers from the thoroughfare to the center of the receiving tracks will double the number of receiving tracks for short trains. (Fig. 7, Chapter 7.)

11.32 Departure Tracks

An outgoing train is made up on a departure track. For most model railroad yards, receiving and departure tracks are usually dual-purpose tracks, even in the large terminals. (Fig. 7, Chapter 7.) Long trains stopping only for a change of crews or perhaps locomotives normally enter and depart from the same track.

The same as receiving tracks, departure tracks should be one train-length long. The alternatives available for receiving tracks to handle longer trains apply also to departure tracks. In Fig. 9, as noted above, two of the tracks of the departure yard extend through the receiving yard for handling trains longer than 35' (10.7m).

11.33 Classification

An important yard function is classification of cars according to destination. Very small yards use any available track for the purpose but larger yards have special classification tracks, often a major yard in itself. Classification yards are covered in Section 11.4.

11.34 Local-Order Tracks

After classification, the cars for the local freights are placed in station order, i.e., arranged so they can be set out without additional working of the train, using local-order tracks. In small yards any available track will be used to 'shake out' a train but at busy yards two or three special tracks may be provided as shown in Figs. 9 and 12.

11.35 Running Tracks

There must be at least one clear track to allow a locomotive to move freely. In small yards the main track or a siding may suffice but larger yards usually require one or more thoroughfare tracks as seen in Figs. 9 and 12 as well as Fig. 7, Chapter 7. Service tracks, such as caboose tracks, often lead from thoroughfares.

11.36 Leads

Wherever switching moves will block traffic unduly, a special track called a lead is provided. A lead is often found at classification yards, see Fig. 10 but may be used anywhere including at small stations (Fig. 2B, Chapter 8).

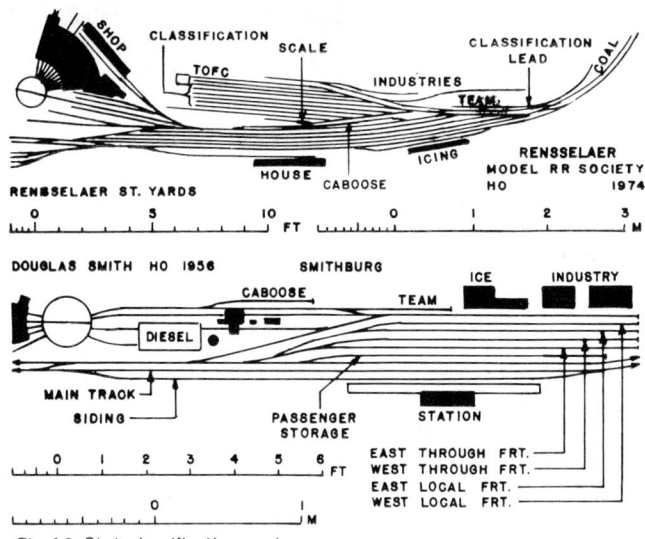

Fig. 10 Stub classification yards

11.37 Turning Tracks

Turning tracks, most often a wye, are particularly useful if end-ramp TOFC or autorack terminals are nearby as in Fig. 9. Combining the wye with a branch-line junction as shown saves space. See Fig. 18, Chapter 7 for other types of turning tracks.

11.38 Storage

In small yards cars temporarily idle or being held may be placed on any available track but in larger yards or in busy small yards storage tracks are added to keep such cars out of the way. In contrast with the other yards such as receiving, storage yards can be stub without operating disadvantage (Figs. 9 and 12).

11.39 Repair and Service Tracks

All but the smallest yards should have a repair track. Although, on a model, repairs are not made at such tracks, they serve as a realistic destination for bad-order cars which can still be moved. Repair tracks are an important part of large classification yards on the prototype.

Among the service tracks which may appear at a yard are locomotive servicing and terminals (Chapter 12), also icing, scale, and transfer tracks (Section 11.5).

11.4 CLASSIFICATION YARDS

Classification yards are most efficient if they have a separate track for each class of car such as westbound local, westbound through, and local drill. The tracks usually are not of the same length as each need hold only the number of cars of that class classified before they are removed to a departure track or taken by a drill. If space allows, classification yards should be double ended to permit simultaneous classification and removal.

Large prototype yards usually have separate classification yards for each direction but this is difficult to justify on a model. The model yard shown in Fig. 6, Chapter 13 has an east and a west yard. Separate tracks for each direction are virtually a must, if the yard is to be effective.

On the prototype, classification yards are usually operated with free-rolling cars. In 1976 either the cars were pushed over a hump, accelerated by gravity after which they rolled into the proper position or they were accelerated by a locomotive and 'kicked' into the proper track. Prior to World War I the locomotive sometimes moved on a parallel track accelerating the cars by a pole pushing the last car of a cut.

Sometimes the pole was mounted on a special poling car. Such yards were called a poling yard. Another old practice was a gravity yard in which the entire yard was on a grade and all switching was by gravity.

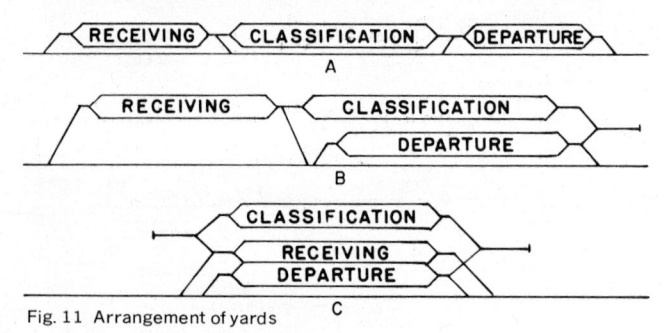

Fig. 11 Arrangement of yards

The most logical arrangement of a classification yard is on a line between the receiving and departure yard as indicated in Fig. 11A. Seldom does space on a model permit such a length. The next best arrangement is with the departure yard in parallel with the classification yard as at B, an example is (1976) the large Meadows (N.J.) yard of Conrail. A lead should be provided for the switching moves from classification to departure. A model example of a yard laid out in this manner is given in Fig. 9. Although the receiving yard could have been placed in parallel with the classification yard, this is less satisfactory as more cars move directly from receiving to classification than from classification to departure.

Most model yards are laid out as in Fig. 11C with the classification, receiving, and departure tracks in parallel. Figs. 10, 12, and 14 contain examples of such yards. Receiving and departure tracks should be double ended if possible for convenient handling of locomotive and caboose. In general parallel receiving and departure tracks are treated as combined tracks but in Fig. 12 they are specified separately as these yards terminate a right-hand running four-track line.

Stub classification tracks, as in Fig. 10, save space as only one ladder and lead are required. For a flat yard handled by a single switcher, little is lost by the use of a stub classification yard.

Hump Yards

Prototype hump yards, North American practice, tend to be large as flat switching is more economical for small yards. Nevertheless many model hump yards have been built, some very small. Hump yards have proven to be a center of visitor interest on layouts which operate for the public.

The chief problem with model hump yards is the fact noted earlier that momentum and friction do not scale properly. There is no possible profile of a model hump which, by gravity alone, will cause cars to duplicate the slow, ponderous rolling of cars on a prototype hump. The model hump yards built to the date of writing have used grades which would assure the cars rolled and just lived with the type of car movements which resulted. Vibrating

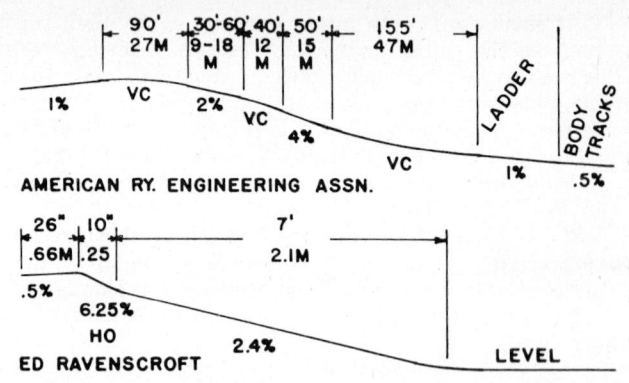

Fig. 13 Hump yard profiles

conveyer techniques are planned for the hump yard of Fig. 9 to achieve slow, even movement but this had not yet been tested in 1975. Fig. 13 shows a prototype and a model hump elevation.

A second problem is suitable retarders. In 1955 T.W.J. Percy reported using electromagnets operating on steel axles or on added magnetic material. Ed Ravenscroft developed an air jet retarder later used by the NYSME. Apparently most model hump yards did not use retarders.

Fig. 14 shows three model hump yards. In all cases, for public shows at least, selected matched cars were humped and rehumped.

Typically the first switch down from the hump on the ladder is a three-way switch on the prototype. The Cedar Hill Yard of the New Haven had a succession of three three-way switches on the route to any body track.

Provision should be made for removing cars from the cut which should not be humped; i.e., autorack cars. In the yards shown in Fig. 14 such screening must be done by pre-humping flat switching in the receiving yard. In Fig. 9 four flat classification tracks are provided for direct use by the hump switcher pushing the cars from the receiving track.

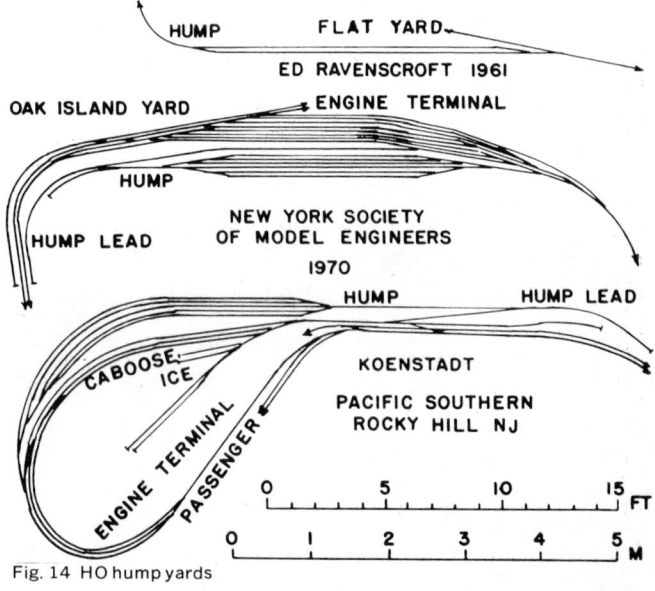

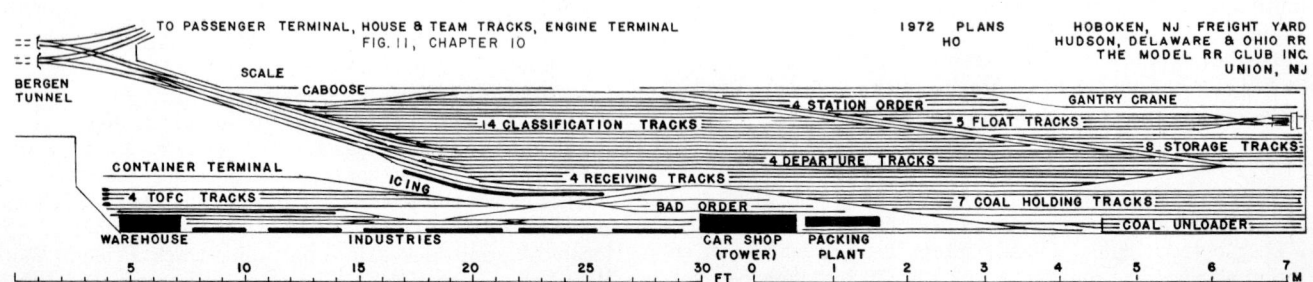

Fig. 14 HO hump yards

Fig. 12 Large model freight yard

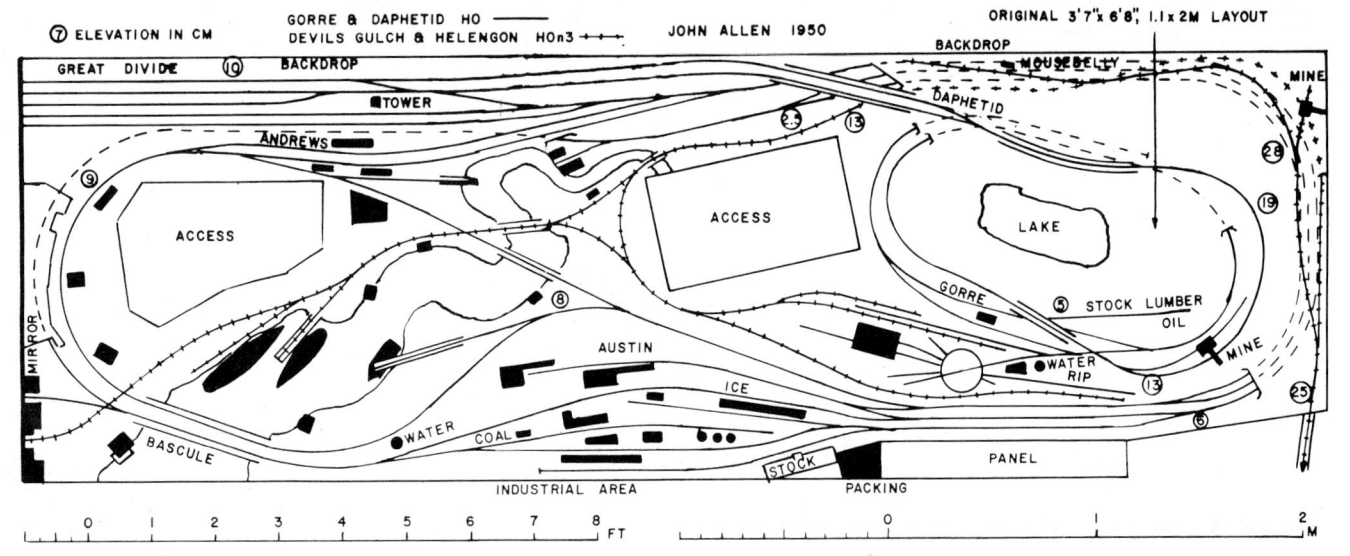

Fig. 15 Home layout with freight destinations

11.5 SERVICE TRACKS

Service tracks should lead from ladders, thoroughfares, sidings, or main tracks and not from tracks which might be blocked by cars. They should be located to minimize the distance cars must be moved to use the services. Space limitations often force a compromise but, during the preliminary design phase, yard moves should be studied to see if an optimum location has been found.

Caboose Tracks

Caboose tracks, unless freight trains operate in only one direction, should be double ended to avoid having to run around a caboose. The logical location for a caboose track is near the yard office. Caboose tracks can be seen in Figs. 9, 10, and 12. In Fig. 7, Chapter 7, two caboose tracks have been provided as this is an interchange yard between the HD&O and the B&O so each railroad requires a separate track to avoid excessive switching.

Icing Tracks

Icing tracks for refrigerator cars are best if double ended. This facilitates an operating rule that refrigerator cars shall be sent to the icing platform for a specific length of time. Because the icing platform is at the height of the car roofs, space can be saved by building it against a hillside. In Fig. 9 the icing platform is against the hump, in Fig. 7, Chapter 7 against a hillside. Other icing tracks can be seen in Figs. 10 and 12.

Track Scale

Unless some other method is used for determining the charges, loaded cars must be weighed for billing purposes before they leave the originating road. Thus a scale can be used to generate additional operating moves by requiring all cars originating from on-line shippers to pass over track scales.

Scales may be placed at any point where they will expedite car movements but, on a model, usually only the major yard justifies a scale.

If the road originates much traffic, a scale on the lead to the classification yard is often installed as shown in Figs. 9 and 12. Such scales are often equipped with gantlet track so cars not to be weighed and the locomotive do not pass over the rails on the scale (Fig. 27, Chapter 6). On the other hand, if only an occasional car must be weighed, the scale might be placed on a separate track as in Fig. 10.

Transfer Tracks

When two non-interchanging railways are modeled such as standard and narrow gauge or a railroad and an interurban line which cannot handle railroad cars, freight transfer tracks provide useful destinations for the cars of both lines. Transfer tracks can be arranged in pairs so freight can be moved directly from one car to another. A traveling or gantry crane is useful on the prototype and an interesting addition on the model.

A transfer platform between the tracks of the two lines is another possibility (Fig. 3, Chapter 14).

When LCL was a major business, transfer tracks and transfer sheds were sometimes provided so cargoes could be transferred between cars without interfering with the operations in the freight house.

11.6 EXAMPLE

Fig. 15 shows the second layout built by John Allen. It was one of the earliest layouts to feature many destinations for freight cars. His first layout was incorporated into the second as indicated. If not the first, this layout was certainly one of the first to take advantage of a large mirror to double the apparent area of scenery. Being surrounded by walls on three sides this layout had a severe problem of access which John Allen corrected on his third and final layout.

CHAPTER 12
SHOPS AND ENGINE TERMINALS

12.1 GENERAL

Engine terminals and shops for cars or locomotives are among the more fascinating features, real or model, of railroads. Since, on a model, there tends to be a large number of locomotives in relation to the number of cars and length of track, sizable engine terminals are installed even on the smaller layouts. Fortunately there are many prototype examples of large engine terminals at relatively small stations, one such being on the Union Pacific at Green River, Wyo. (See Division Points in Chapter 13.) The important thing is to provide all the necessary facilities. For example, if coal-burning steam locomotives are operated, an ash pit is a necessity on the prototype and should not be left out on a model in order to make room for a larger roundhouse.

Shops, in contrast to engine terminals, are not part of the usual operation of a model railroad. Although seldom modeled, they can be effective and interesting as background scenery. Shops can also serve as the destination for bad-order cars which can still be either pushed or pulled, also for locomotives which can still move.

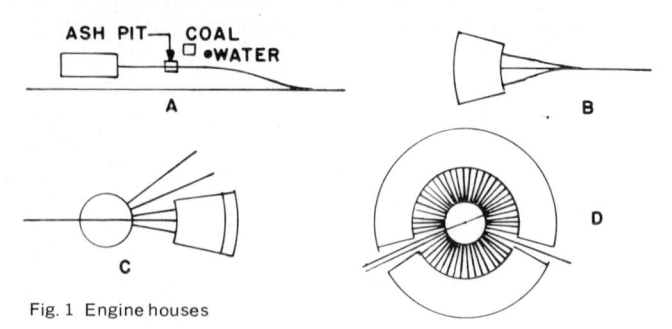

Fig. 1 Engine houses

12.2 ENGINE HOUSE AND TURNTABLE

Small railroads, the Rahway Valley is one, might have one or two-stall engine houses without a turntable as at A in Fig. 1. Although usually rectangular, sometimes such engine houses were fan shaped as at B, see also Fig. 6. Small railroads often had as many stalls as they had locomotives and so could store their locomotives in the engine house. Large railroads typically used engine houses for inspection, maintenance, and light repairs only, locomotives being stored on open track. On the model, engine houses tend to be large with respect to the rest of the railroad and using them for storage protects locomotives from dust.

In steam days most engine houses were equipped with a turntable. Some busy terminals had two turntables to speed operation. In many cases turntables were still in use for diesels in 1974. There were, however, railroads such as the New Jersey, Indiana & Illinois in South Bend which removed the turntable and replaced it with the turnout fan as in Fig. 1B for the stalls still in service.

Usually open tracks were provided from the turntable in addition to roundhouse stalls as at C in Fig. 1 but large engine terminals sometimes had full-circle engine houses as at D, in some cases even two full circles. Except for small scales such as N, full-circle engine houses present an access problem if modeled.

Most engine houses are located at central points where locomotives are serviced such as at terminals and division points. Nevertheless they may be placed as needed. Near Mobile, Alabama, the AT&N had, at its transfer bridge, a one-locomotive engine house just large enough to house a small diesel switcher.

It is most convenient if stall tracks are directly opposite the approach tracks to the turntable as at C and D in Fig. 1. Often, however, the space available calls for a different location.

Most modelers prefer a turntable long enough to handle the largest locomotive which might ever operate on that layout rather than restricting the locomotive types which can use the turntable. Fig. 2 shows the length of table required to handle the longest steam locomotive ever built. As indicated in that figure, the table should be somewhat longer than the overall wheelbase to eliminate the need for

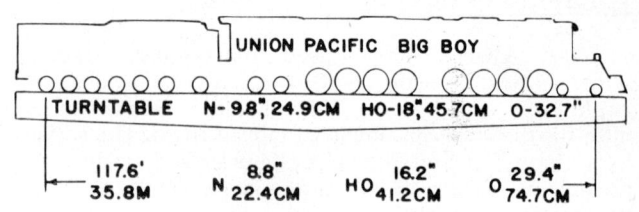

Fig. 2 Longest locomotive

precise spotting on the table. Most Pacifics and Consolidations can be handled on a 72' (22m) table which is 5.5" (14cm) in N, 10" (25.4cm) in HO, and 18.1" (46cm) in O scale.

The distance from the pit to the doors of the roundhouse depends upon the space available and the number of stalls desired. The controlling dimension is the width of doorway required, 13 scale feet (4m) being as close clearance as is feasible. Often more stalls can be included by making some shorter as at A in Fig. 3. A nice scenic effect is to model the roundhouse as if the shorter stalls were an older first roundhouse with the longer stalls a later addition.

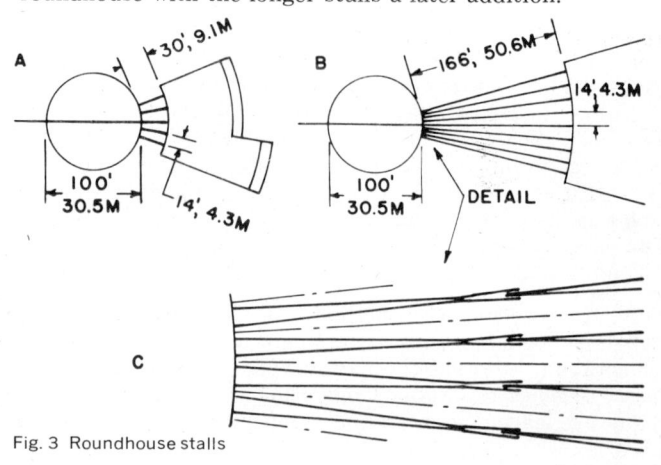

Fig. 3 Roundhouse stalls

More stalls can be included by extending the distance between the turntable pit and the roundhouse as at B in Fig. 3. In this case the distance is such that the stall tracks overlap as shown in the detail. Such overlap with the required frogs was not common but there were many examples, Janesville, Wis. on the Milwaukee for one. For small engine houses the stall tracks may curve into a rectangular house, a model example is given in Fig. 3, Chapter 14.

Most prototype roundhouses have an extension beyond the stall tracks, often with a lower roof for passage of workers, material, and machines. Even if such a passage is

58

Chapter 12

modeled, by running the stall tracks to the roundhouse wall, the building can be made smaller if space is pressing. Further, it is not necessary to make the stalls deep enough to enclose completely the longest locomotive. It was not uncommon in steam days to see the last few feet of the tank of the long locomotives extending from the roundhouse stall doorway.

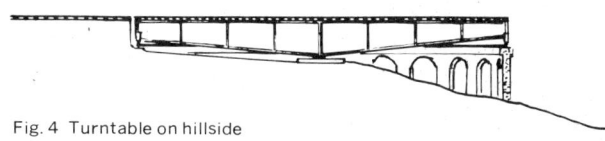

Fig. 4 Turntable on hillside

Turntables were often found without engine houses for the purpose of turning locomotives at a terminal or helper locomotives at the end of a grade. Two model examples are illustrated in Fig. 24, Chapter 7. If such turntables are on an upper level, it may make for more realistic scenery if only a partial pit is modeled with the ground falling away on one side as shown in Fig. 4. Prototype examples of such pits were rare but existed, one on the Western Maryland.

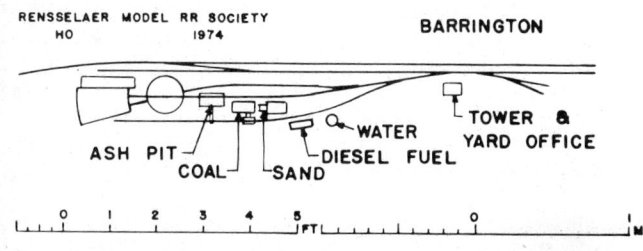

Fig. 5 Engine terminal

12.3 LOCOMOTIVE SERVICING

Inspection Pits

Unless locomotives are always run into a roundhouse with pits, the usual first stop of an incoming locomotive is at the inspection pits. This is particularly true of diesel and electric locomotives.

Ash Pits

Coal-burning locomotives require an ash pit. If inspection pits are provided, the ash pit (sometimes called cinder pit) customarily is between the inspection pit and the turntable. In most cases ash pits have an adjacent service track for ash-removal cars. In the case of open-side hand-shoveled pits, the ash removal track was often depressed as can be seen in the top engine terminal of Fig. 6. On a model, due to space considerations, this track often services the coaling tower and the sand house as well. An example can be seen in Fig. 5, also in Figs. 7, Chapter 7. Ash pits were sometimes placed for use by through locomotives, for example at the end of station platforms.

Fuel

Coal-burning locomotives require some form of coaling station. A small engine terminal might use a locomotive crane which could also be used to empty the ash pits. Western railroads, in particular, often had an elevated track from which coal could be shoveled or dumped into bins, see the top example in Fig. 6. Modelers tend to use a mechanical coaling plant in which coal is raised from a hopper under the service track by a conveyor or other mechanical means. Such plants require the minimum area. The prototype sometimes placed a loading hopper under the locomotive service track thus saving even more space.

Locomotives normally took coal on arriving at a terminal so the most convenient location for the coaling station was where a locomotive could be coaled while it was standing over the inspection or ash pit.

Oil-burning and diesel locomotives normally are fueled by hoses. The major model details for such service is the oil storage tank and the pump house, see the middle example of Fig. 6.

Fueling stations, particularly for diesels, were often located where they could service through locomotives.

Sand Houses

All locomotives require sand. In steam-locomotive days customarily a sand house with a sand dryer was provided, located, if possible, so the sand box could be filled while the locomotive was over the inspection or ash pit. Diesel terminals most often have sand towers.

Water

All locomotives require water but steam locomotives required it in large quantities. Usually a large water tank was a prominent feature of an engine terminal. This tank might service the locomotives directly from a spout on its discharge pipe but, in more modern practice, the water was delivered through standpipes, also called water columns or water cranes. A convenient location for the standpipe permitted the locomotive to take water while standing over the ash pit.

An important detail which can be added on a model is a pump house and water-treatment building.

Wash Racks

Wash racks, consisting of well-drained wood or concrete platforms, if provided, normally service incoming locomotives. They may be provided with elevated platforms.

12.4 MISCELLANEOUS FACILITIES

Boiler House

A boiler house (providing steam for heating, sand drying, and for maintaining pressure in locomotive and

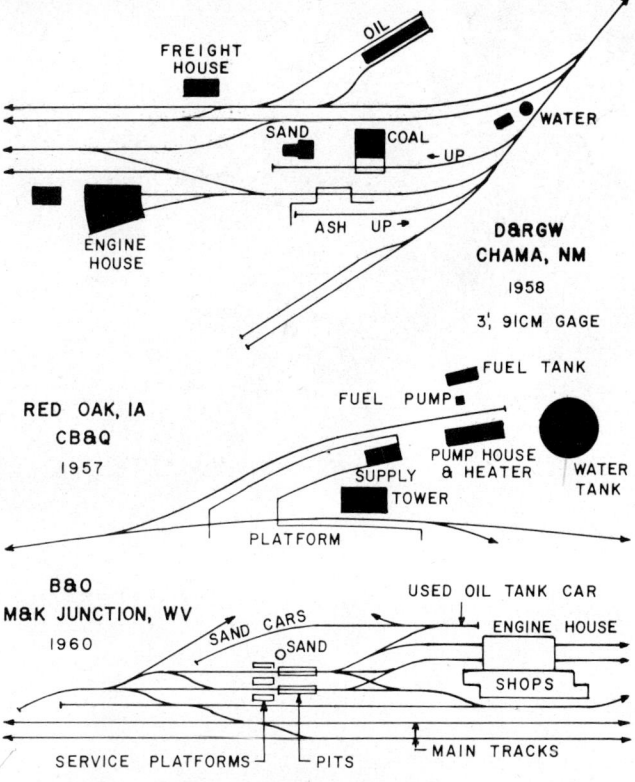

Fig. 6 Small prototype engine terminals

Chapter 12   59

wrecker boilers) was often built near or attached to the engine house. Sometimes electrical generators were included.

Fan House

Fans were sometimes provided to ventilate the engine house and for forced draft. These fans were usually located in small buildings adjacent to the engine house. In rare cases smoke jacks (similar in appearance to water standpipes) were installed on open tracks, their intakes could be placed over the stacks of locomotives for smoke control.

Oil House

Lubricating oil and waste was often stored in a separate building near the engine house.

Offices and Locker Rooms

A building connected to or near the engine house was usually provided for offices, locker rooms, and other personnel facilities.

Wrecker

When a track for storing a wrecker was provided, it customarily was placed near the engine house for maintenance and steam. A model example can be seen in Fig. 9, Chapter 11.

Elm Grove enginehouse on Allen McClelland's famed Virginian & Ohio Railroad is used jointly by the V&O and the connecting KC&B shortline. Skillful blending of two plastic kits resulted in a custom looking enginehouse not otherwise available. Rail is code 70.

12.5 SHOPS

Light repair work on locomotives may be accomplished in a roundhouse and on street cars in a portion of a car barn. Repair tracks are an essential part of large classification yards. Large passenger terminals often had a rip track and wheel pit for light repairs on passenger cars (Fig. 11 Chapter 10). Heavy repairs, however, require special facilities including a crane. Therefore specially-equipped shops were found on all but the smallest railroads. Even the 11 mile (18km) Raritan River RR, a short line, had a sizable shop building at South Amboy, NJ. Small shops might handle both cars and locomotives but more often separate facilities were provided. On large railroads there might be a major shop at some central location, e.g. at Roanoke on the N&W, and smaller shops at terminals or division points.

Although shop buildings make interesting models, particularly if equipped with a working transfer table, they do not contribute significantly to operational interest so large shops are seldom modeled. Fig. 10, Chapter 11 shows a small shop modeled adjacent to a roundhouse. A space-saving approach is shown in Fig. 9, Chapter 11 where the tracks approaching the shop and the shop front is modeled but the bulk of the shop appears in a backdrop. Additional information on shops may be found in NMRA Data Sheets D3j.03-.06.

Large model railroads might have special shops such as the MU repair building in Fig. 11, Chapter 10.

CHAPTER 13
JUNCTIONS AND DIVISION POINTS

13.1 GENERAL

Junction

A junction is a point where two or more railroads or lines of the same railroad join or cross. Prototype junctions range from a single switch or crossing to complex trackage incorporating auxiliary tracks for operating flexibility.

Division Point

Except for the smallest, railroads are divided into divisions for operation and maintenance. In steam days it was not uncommon to change locomotives and cabooses at division points, the divisions acting in many ways as though they were separate railroads. Sometimes the same train number would be used for two or more different trains if they were in different divisions. For example in 1905 on the PRR No. 1 was both a N.Y. to Pittsburgh train and also a Louisville to Chicago train.

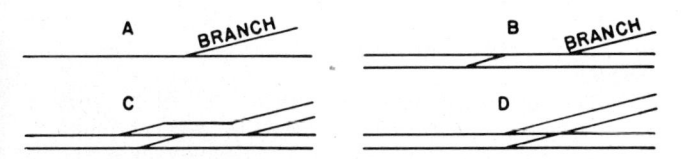

Fig. 1 Simple junctions

13.2 JUNCTIONS

Distances on model railroads are necessarily short therefore junctions are always in or close to stations or yards. Consequently it is practical to install simple junctions such as those shown in Fig. 1. Any set outs or drilling which must be done can be accomplished at the nearest yard or station.

The simplest junction with a choice of route is a turnout as at A in Fig. 1. If one of the lines is double track, a crossover is installed as at B. Even if one of the routes is a busy multiple-track main and there is frequent traffic to and from the branch, a junction of the type shown at B may be found with additional crossovers between the remaining tracks of the multiple-track line. One example is at Hunter tower on the PC (1975) where frequent commuter trains of the CRRNJ operating over a single-track line join the four-track ex-Pennsylvania main.

For simple double-track junctions, the arrangement at C in Fig. 1 is common in North American railroad practice. That at D is more typical of rapid transit and street car lines, also in Europe, particularly Great Britain for railroads.

In dense traffic areas, even as late as 1974, it was common practice to control junctions with interlocking machines in towers. Therefore a branch might parallel the main until an interlocking was reached. Fig. 2 shows an example on the DL&W, the junction being at a three-track station and having a double set of crossovers for flexibility. Junctions at stations are not uncommon and save space on a model. The junction shown in Fig. 2 was actually built to full scale size on two different HO layouts.

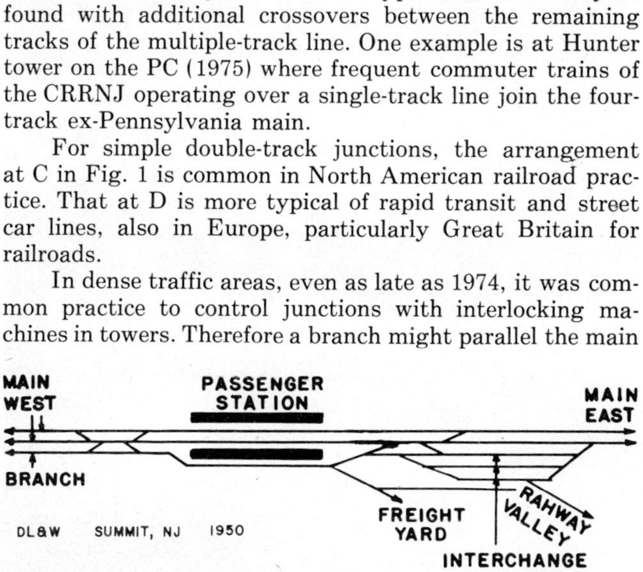

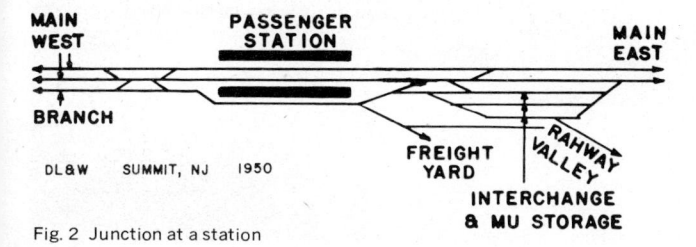

When a junction is remote from a station or yard, either in fact or in concept, auxiliary tracks may be provided where cars can be left either for the next train down the other line or for leaving the cars destined for the main line while the crew works the branch.

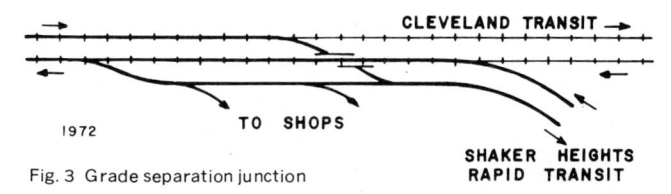

Fig. 3 Grade separation junction

The junctions shown thus far have been flat, that is all the tracks are at the same grade. Most prototype junctions are of this type including some serving busy multi-track main lines such as in Chicago where the Milwaukee leaving Union Station crosses the tracks leaving the C&NW terminal. There are, nevertheless, many prototype junctions with grade separations to permit the diverging or crossing route to cross over or under main tracks (sometimes called 'flying' junctions). Perhaps the most famous of these is the Zoo interlocking in Philadelphia, a Y junction with several tracks on each leg of the wye. Rapid transit tends to use grade-separation junctions more often than do railroads although flat junctions are the rule in Chicago. Fig. 3 shows a rapid-transit junction in Cleveland. The left-hand running on joint trackage permits the doors of the Shaker Heights cars to face the center platforms.

On a model considerable space is required to separate the grades (Section 6.6) and operation is less interesting. Unless a grade-separation is to be a scenic feature, it is better to use flat junctions. An exception is where lines simply cross with no interconnection.

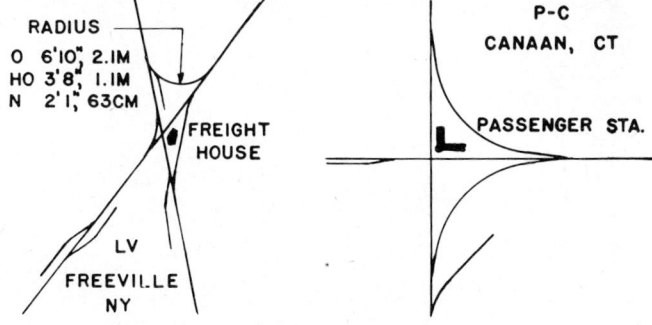

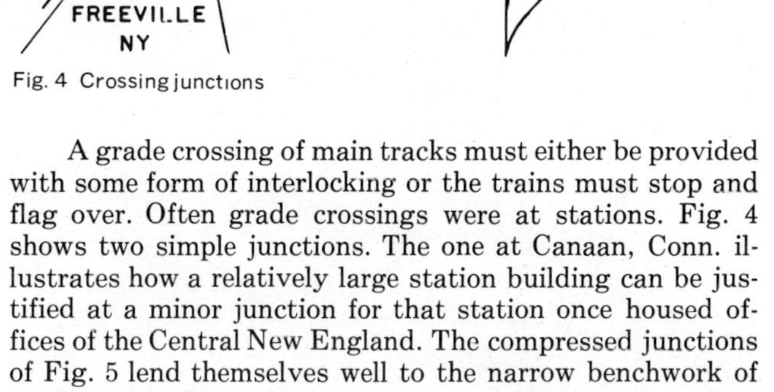

Fig. 2 Junction at a station

Fig. 4 Crossing junctions

A grade crossing of main tracks must either be provided with some form of interlocking or the trains must stop and flag over. Often grade crossings were at stations. Fig. 4 shows two simple junctions. The one at Canaan, Conn. illustrates how a relatively large station building can be justified at a minor junction for that station once housed offices of the Central New England. The compressed junctions of Fig. 5 lend themselves well to the narrow benchwork of model railroads.

Chapter 13   61

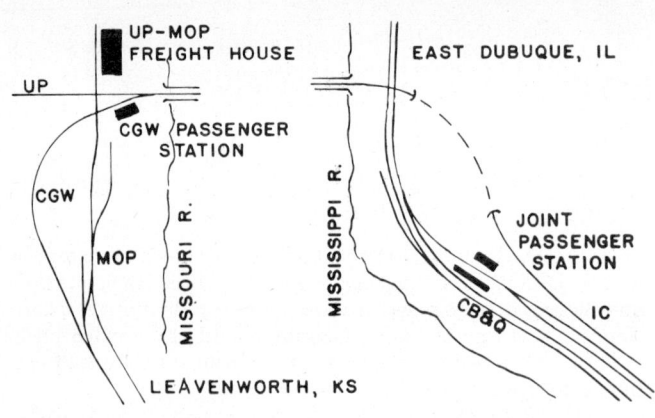

Fig. 5 Compressed junctions

Some junctions are Y because trains operate from any approaching track to any other but even where a Y is not required for train operation, a junction gives the opportunity to add a turning wye with little increased need for space. The junctions of Fig. 4 contain wyes as does the junction between the main and a branch in Fig. 9, Chapter 11. In the latter case the wye was designed into the junction for the sole purpose of turning moves.

13.3 DIVISION POINTS

If the intent is to have much working of the train, changing of locomotives and the like in contrast to picking up and setting out cars, a division point is a logical choice for a main, or perhaps the only, station on the layout. Particularly on western railroads, division points were often located far from population centers so there was little if any local switching and passenger stops were primarily for servicing the trains. A large engine terminal can be justified for an otherwise small station and yard by the concept that the faster but lighter locomotives coming in from the plains are replaced on all trains by heavier locomotives for the mountains ahead. A main track and siding, two or three receiving-departure tracks, a caboose track and perhaps a short auxiliary track or two are all that would be needed in addition to engine facilities to create an active division point as each train through would require action.

Division points are logical locations for classification yards and the model division point of Fig. 6 has two, one east and one west. Having two small yards is a questionable use of space for it is impractical to operate more than one classification switcher in a small yard. The much larger division point shown in Fig. 9, Chapter 11 has only one classification yard.

Service tracks such as icing and stock resting also are logically located at division points. Some of these facilities appear in the two figures cited above.

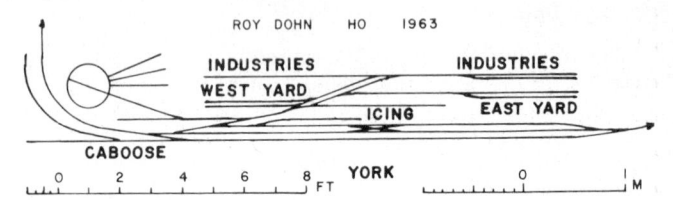

Fig. 6 Model division point

Division points with all the facilities listed above are also found at major cities and there would have local switching in addition. In such a case the station could be operated either as a division point or as a station midway on a division without change of design, only operating methods.

The point separating two divisions is not necessarily a yard or special facility. For example in 1966 the Philadelphia and New York Divisions of the Pennsylvania met at mile post 76 (Holmes interlocking).

Bob Hegge's Crooked Mountain Lines is a superb example of an O scale trolley line with power being provided from an overhead catenary to the locomotives via pantographs. Great model railroads have been built in all of the popular scales and many top modelers have discovered the extra fun that comes from modeling one of the variations of standard model railroading: traction, heavy electrics, narrow gauge, foreign, or old time railroading.

Chapter 13

CHAPTER 14
TRACTION AND SPECIAL RAILWAYS

14.1 GENERAL

Some special railways, that is railways other than standard-gauge railroad common carriers, have short radii and therefore are more easily modelable in a restricted area. Any special railway, if built in conjunction with a model of a standard railroad, enhances the scenic effect, provides a contrast to conventional track and trains, and adds interesting operating features.

14.2 TRACTION

Traction can be divided into five categories, electrified railroads, interurbans, street cars, rapid transit and mine/industrial. All categories have the added scenic feature of the overhead wire or third rail even if the locomotives or cars operate two-rail. That added conductor can be exploited for independent control. See the Model Traction Handbook, coauthored by the author of this Handbook and published by Vane Jones, 6710 Hampton Dr. E., Indianapolis, IN 46226 for detailed information.

Electrified Railroads

Except for motive power, electrified railroads are essentially the same as steam/diesel railroads. The impact of electrification on design is primarily on engine facilities and storage yards for MU trains. Such matters are covered in the appropriate chapters. Seldom, however, are model railroads totally electrified. If not, the concept should in-

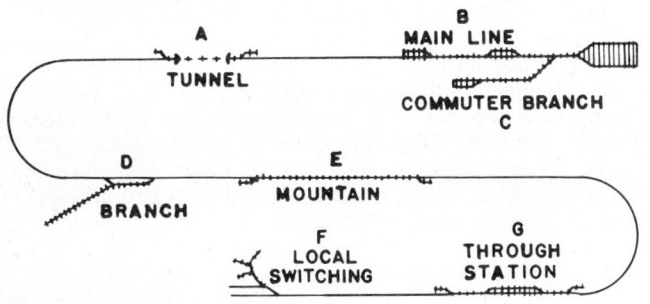

Fig. 1 Railroad electrification

clude the type and extent of electrification. Fig. 1 illustrates some of the more common applications of electrification to parts of a steam/diesel railroad.

Several prototype examples existed where electric locomotives pulled steam-drawn trains through tunnels as at A in Fig. 1: Hoosac Tunnel on the B&M for one. The Chatham, N.J., HO Club had such a tunnel in which the electrics operated from the overhead wire outside the tunnel to gain independent control but ran two-rail in the tunnel to avoid stringing wire where it could not be seen.

At B main-line electrification out from a terminal is indicated. Such electrification may be just for MU commuter trains as on the DL&W and IC or for through trains in addition as on the PRR and New Haven. The latter requires locomotive-changing facilities at the end of electrification. Electrification may include a branch as at C even when all branches are not electrified, again the DL&W was an example.

An electrified branch may be independent of an electrified main and remote from a terminal as at D, as on the Erie and on the New Haven. Also a section of the mainline might be electrified, E, usually because of heavy grades as on the Virginian, N&W, and CMSt.P&P.

Electrification can be applied to a through station as at G in Fig. 1 to keep steam locomotives out of the passenger station: Cleveland. Also for smoke abatement the local switching may be electric as at F. The West Side freight line in New York was operated by three-power locomotives, a diesel charging storage batteries was used for switching non-electrified spurs.

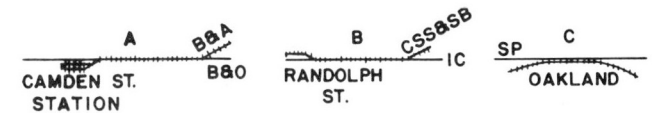

Fig. 2 Interurban railroad passenger stations

Interurban

As a means of adding operating interest, an interurban line is probably the most effective special railway which can be added to a standard railroad. Prototype interurban lines interchanged freight with railroads as well as operated passenger cars in coordination with railroad passenger trains. The interurban may share tracks with and even stations with the railroad. Examples are shown in Fig. 2. The Baltimore & Annapolis operated over B&O tracks and used the B&O Camden Station in Baltimore as at A. Similarly the South Shore still (1976) uses the IC tracks and some through stations on entering Chicago but has a separate head station at Randolph St. as at B. In some cases the interurban and the railroad shared the same station but had entirely different tracks, at Oakland, C, the SP tracks were on the lower level, the interurban on the upper.

It is interchanging of freight rather than passenger service which makes an interurban line such a desirable addition to a model railroad. See Section 11.2, Foreign Interchange, for more information and examples of prototype and model traction interchanges.

Although the design of a model interurban line is basically similar to the design of any model railroad and some of the information specific to interurbans is given in this Handbook, space does not permit complete descriptions of typical interurban practice. See the reference cited in the first paragraph of this Section.

Street Cars

A working street-car line makes an attractive scenic addition to a model railroad, even non-operating tracks modeled in the street with overhead wire makes the scene more interesting. If the street-car system is part of an interurban line, its tracks can be used for interchange freight as in Sacramento by the Sacramento Northern which increases operational possibilities. The street car system itself could do some terminal switching of freight cars as was done in Kansas City. The tracks used for interchange freight must not be of minimum street-car radii (Fig. 2, Chapter 6). However it is feasible to limit the length of cars which can be sent through interchange to a street-car line.

Rapid Transit

Rapid transit lines are primarily mass carriers of passengers. Elevated lines in particular are interesting additions to model railroad systems even if the rapid transit is dummy or perhaps just one station with the trains simply leaving and returning. An example of a subway rapid transit system included in the plans of an HO scale railroad is given in Fig. 23 Chapter 7. There were examples, nevertheless, of railroad interchange freight on rapid transit lines in Chicago and New York.

Mine/Industrial

Mine railways bringing coal from a mine to a breaker are a natural addition to model railroads (Fig. 5, Chapter 11). From an operating point of view, the most useful industrial traction lines are those handling standard-gauge cars received from the railroad. Power plants sometimes had such electrified lines. One in Chicago used underrunning third rail, one in Toledo direct suspension. Steel mills, automobile plants, also a small manufacturer's railway serving several industries are possibilities.

14.3 NARROW GAUGE

Since the various narrow-gauge railways did not interconnect except on a very limited basis, no standard practices or even gauge evolved. If the main railway of a model is to be narrow gauge, it is important that a specific prototype such as the D&RGW or, at least, a general prototype such as the Maine two-footers be selected and the model made consistent with that prototype. However most, perhaps all, narrow gauge lines had a connection with a standard-gauge railroad where freight was transferred. Even if a working standard gauge model is not to be constructed, including the connection station adds scenic interest and serves as an excellent generator of freight loads as well as a logical terminal for the narrow-gauge passenger trains.

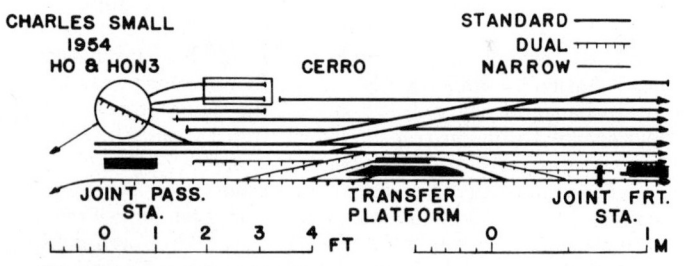

Fig. 3 Dual gauge terminal

When both standard and narrow gauge lines are operational, it is important that both are built to be of the same period. If the standard gauge line is set in the modern era, the narrow gauge line should appear to have survived to that time and not operating in the past (Section 2.4).

If the narrow gauge line is a common-carrier, both the standard and the narrow gauge could use the same freight house and passenger station. Transfer platforms sometimes were provided to transfer loads without interfering with freight-house activities. Fig. 3 shows a model yard which served both narrow and standard gauge lines as a terminal, the two lines leaving in opposite directions. In this case the common facilities had dual gauge track including the turntable. A separate narrow gauge engine house, to the left of the tracks shown, was provided. It is feasible to keep the two gauges separate for simplicity of track construction (Fig. 15, Chapter 11). However dual gauge track and switches add interest.

Standard gauge cars were sometimes handled in interchange by narrow gauge lines, the East Broad Top for one. That road had special car lifters for interchanging the trucks. In Switzerland in 1974 special cars mounting rails at standard gauge very low to the track were used to carry standard gauge cars on narrow gauge lines.

Bulk cargos such as coal are a logical source of interchange between a narrow and a standard gauge line. Coal must be graded and washed at some point so the narrow gauge hoppers might as well bring mine-run coal to a single plant from which the coal is loaded into standard gauge hoppers. Such a plant was at Mt. Union, Pa. on the East Broad Top.

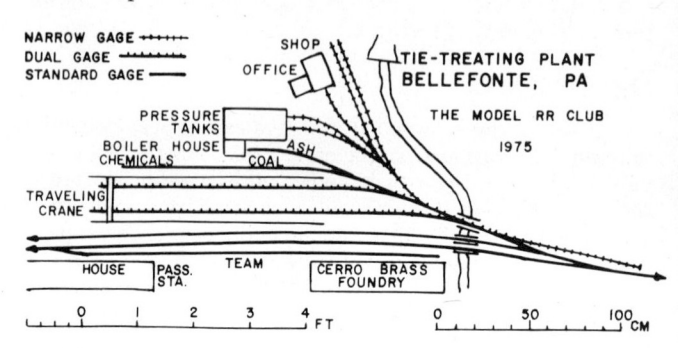

Fig. 4 Tie-treating plant

Some types of industries are well suited for narrow gauge lines, for example the HO scale tie-treating plant shown in Fig. 4. It is based on such a plant once operating in Port Reading, N.J. with steam narrow gauge tank locomotives. Such a plant serves as a destination for several types of cars; gondolas with raw ties and poles, tank cars of creosote, cars with machinery and supplies, and hoppers of coal for the boilers. It originates loads of treated ties and poles plus cars of ash.

Operating narrow gauge lines can be justified for many types of line-side industries. Brick plants can bring the clay in from the pits by narrow gauge. Lima Brick in Ohio was an example. Many industries handling steel or other heavy material had internal narrow gauge systems. The Homestake Gold Mine in Lead, S.D. in 1974 had an extensive dual narrow gauge system.

14.4 LOGGING LINES

Logging railways which bring the timber to a saw mill directly can be narrow gauge. However, if the logs are shipped over a railroad to the saw mill, a standard gauge logging line creates an interesting interchange with the railroad. Some logging lines leading to the Yosemite Valley RR lowered the cars to the interchange by cable down steep grades, a space-saving technique if modeled. Even without cable assist, logging railroads can have very steep grades. In Michigan one grade was so steep that a locomotive could not pull up the grade unless it approached at a high speed (high for a logging line).

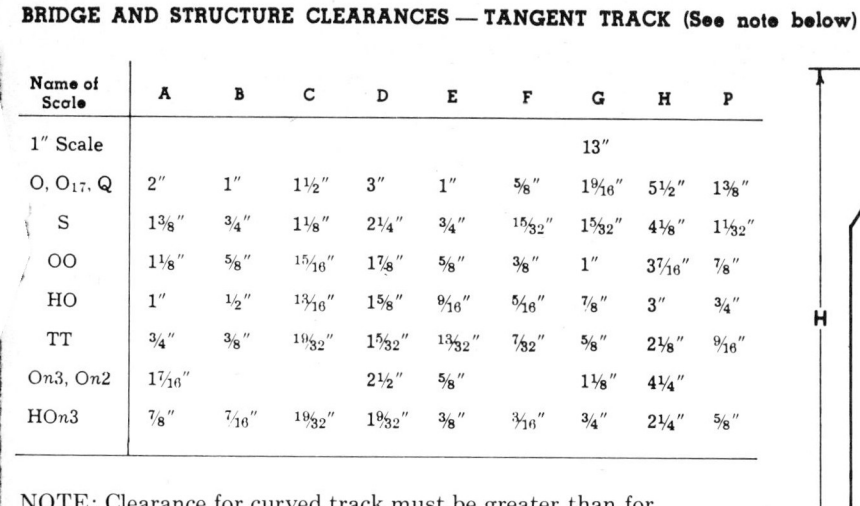

BRIDGE AND STRUCTURE CLEARANCES — TANGENT TRACK (See note below)

Name of Scale	A	B	C	D	E	F	G	H	P
1" Scale							13"		
O, O₁₇, Q	2"	1"	1½"	3"	1"	⅝"	1⁹⁄₁₆"	5½"	1⅜"
S	1⅜"	¾"	1⅛"	2¼"	¾"	¹⁵⁄₃₂"	1⁵⁄₃₂"	4⅛"	1¹⁄₃₂"
OO	1⅛"	⅝"	¹⁵⁄₁₆"	1⅞"	⅝"	⅜"	1"	3⁷⁄₁₆"	⅞"
HO	1"	½"	¹³⁄₁₆"	1⅝"	⁹⁄₁₆"	⁵⁄₁₆"	⅞"	3"	¾"
TT	¾"	⅜"	¹⁹⁄₃₂"	1⁵⁄₃₂"	¹³⁄₃₂"	⁷⁄₃₂"	⅝"	2⅛"	⁹⁄₁₆"
On3, On2	1⁷⁄₁₆"			2½"	⅝"		1⅛"	4¼"	
HOn3	⅞"	⁷⁄₁₆"	¹⁹⁄₃₂"	1⁹⁄₃₂"	⅜"	³⁄₁₆"	¾"	2¼"	⅝"

NOTE: Clearance for curved track must be greater than for tangent track. This greater clearance must gradually ease into the tangent track clearance as long equipment completes its transition from the curve into the tangent.

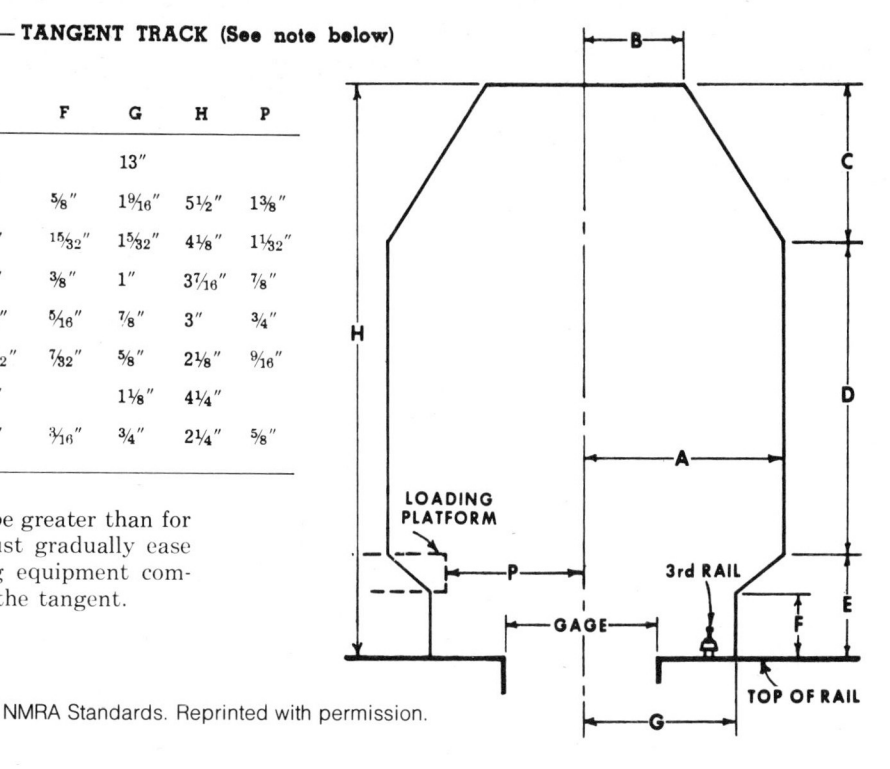

NMRA Standards. Reprinted with permission.

INDEX

Access, Aisles 8
  Duck unders 10
  Reaching distances 8
  To track 8
  Under benchwork 9
  View 8
Access aisle dimensions 8
Allen, John 19, 57
Apron 41
Armstrong, John 10, 14
Ash pit 59
Assumed location 4

Backdrop 4, 14, 17, 18
Backdrop, Dividing 14
Bell Laboratories Model RR Club 12, 38
Belt line 6
Benchwork 3, 8
Benchwork, Access under 9
  Construction 11
  Corners 15
  Depressed section 11
  Design 33
  Duck-unders 10
  Gates 10
  Grid 9
  Hanging 11
  Height 8
  Joist 9, 12, 13
  Movable section 10
  Openings 10
  Peninsular 10
  Permanent 12
  Portable 11, 12
  Reaching distances 8
  Scenic consideration 11
  Serpentine 10
  Shelf 10
  Standards 9
  Stringer 9
  Table-top 9
  Table 10
  Tilted joists 11

Two-level 11
Types 9
Viewing consideration 8
Walkunder 10
Block, Definition 22
Boiler house 59
Braun, H. J. 16

Cab control 20
Caboose track 57
Canal 16
Car destination 52
Car ferry 41
Car float 41
Car service track 51
Central Jersey Model RR Association 41, 47
Chatham Model RR Club 63
Choice of concept 7
Chubb, Bruce 23
Circular curve 25
Classification yard 55
Clearance 32, 44, 65
Clearnace 35
Coaling station 59
Columbus Model RR Club 33
Complementary destinations 53
Compound ladder 37
Concept, Belt line 6
  Bridge line 5
  Choice 7
  Era 5
  Location 4
  Main line 5
  Purpose 4
  Season 5
  Short line 6
  Switching line 6
  Terminal RR 5
  Type of RR 5
Construction sequence 17
Container terminal 54
Control panel 23
Control systems 3, 20

Coupler gathering range 31
Coupler limitations 31
Crossing 29
Crossover 26, 37
Cubic spiral 25
Culvert 17
Curve, Circular 25
  Degree 24
  Easement 25
  Minimum radius 24
  Reverse 26
  Template 35, 44
  Vertical 30
Curved turnout 27

Dean, Lorne 19
Degree of curve 24
Departure track 55
Depressed benchwork 11
Design, Benchwork 33
  Detailed 44, 45
  Preliminary 33
  Sequence 45
Detailed design 44, 45
Diagram, Elevation 40
  Track 40
Diamond 29
Dividing backdrop 4, 14, 18, 42
Division control 20
Division point 61, 62
Dohn, Roy 13, 62
Double ladder 37
Double track 36, 42
Double-track illusion 21
Drainage 17
Drawing scale 45
Duck-unders 10, 11

Easement 25
El Paso Model RR Club 18
Electrical features of design 20
Electrified RR 63
Elevation diagram 40

Appendix

Elevation 35, 40
Engine house 58
Engine terminal 58
Era 5
Escape crossover 48
Expansion 38
Express 50

Fan House 60
Final design 45
Final drawing 46
Float bridge 41
Flying junction 61
Foreign interchange 52
Freight, Destinations 52
  Facilities 52
  House 52
  Yard 54
Frog 26
Ft. Gordon Model RR Club 40, 47
Fueling station 59

Gantlet 29
Gantlet turnout 27
Grade 29, 35
Grid benchwork 9
Grid 35, 46

Hanging benchwork 11
Head station 48
Height of benchwork 8
Hidden yard 41
High benchwork 8
Holding track 53
House track 52
Hump yard 56

Icing track 57
Industrial RR 64
Industrial track 54
Inspection pit 59
Intercept of turnout 27
Interchange 7, 22, 52
Interchange tracks 22, 52
Interlocking 22, 43

Joist 9, 11, 12, 13
Joist spacing 12, 13
Junction 61

Ladder 37
Lap switch 28
Large layout definition 5
Layout size 5
Layout, Portable 12
Layover track 41
Lead, Switching 43, 55
  Turnout 27
L-girder benchwork 12, 13
Limitations, Benchwork 3
  Control systems 3
  Couplers 31
  Maintenance 3
  Manpower 3
Location of RR 4
Local-order track 55
Locomotive servicing 59
Logging RR 64
Low benchwork 8

MU shop 51
Madison Model RR Club 18
Mail 50
Main line 5
Main track 35, 36
Maintenance 3
Medium layout definition 5
Mine RR 64
Minimum radius 24
Mirror 15, 16, 17, 18, 19

Modular design 38
Movable benchwork 13
Movable-point frog 26

Narrow gauge 64
New York Society of Model Engineers
  14, 47, 48, 50, 56

Oil house 60
Openings through benchwork 10
Out-and-back 33
Oval 42
Overhang 32, 44

Pacific Southern Model RR Club 41, 56
Panel, Control 23
Passenger, Facilities 47
  Platforms 47
  Stations 47
  Yards 50
Pass the buck control 20
Patterson, Richard C. 41
Peninsular benchwork 10
Percent of grade 30
Percy, T. W. J. 56
Piggyback 53
Platform cover 49
Point-to-point 33
Portable benchwork 12
Portable layout 12
Prefabricated track 44
Preliminary design 33
Produce terminal 52
Prototype location 4
Public shows 4
Pullman service track 51
Purpose of layout 4

Rabit-warren benchwork 10
Ramsdell, Roger 15
Rapid transit 63
Ravenscroft, Ed 56
Receiving track 54
Rensselaer Model RR Society 14, 18, 48,
  49, 54, 55, 59
Repair track 55
Reverse curve 26
Reversing loop 21, 37
Reversing track 37
River 15, 16
Roundhouse 58
Running track 55

Sacks, David 40
Sacremento Model RR Club 19
Sand house 59
Scenery, Backdrop 4, 14, 17, 18, 42
  Basics 14
  Canal 16
  Corners 15
  Culverts 17
  Dividers 14, 18
  Drainage 17
  Mirrors 15, 16, 17, 18, 19
  Rivers 15
  Signals 22
  Streams 15
  Trestles 18
Section, Definition 22
  X Section 22
Sectional track 44
Sectionalization 22
Selective compression 14
Sequence of construction 17
Sequence of design 45
Serpentine benchwork 10
Service track 55, 57, 59
Shelf benchwork 10
Shop 58, 60
Short line 6
Show loop 40

Side station 47
Siding 35, 36
Signal, Interlocking 22
  Wayside 22
Simple ladder 37
Single-station operation 42
Slip switch 28
Small layout definition 5
Small layouts 42, 44
Small, Charles 64
Smith, Douglas 55
Spiral 25
Split ladder 37
Standards, Benchwork 9
  Checking 46
  Clearance 32, 65
  Grade 30
  Radius 24
  Reaching distance 9
  Track centers 32
  Trackwork 24
  Turnouts 27
Station, Combination 47
  Design 49
  Freight 52
  Fuel 59
  Head 48
  Passenger 47
  Platform cover 49
  Side 47
  Throat 49
  Through 47
Storage 55
Storage track 53
Straight turnout 27
Stringer 9, 13
Street car 63
Stub station 48
Summit-New Providence HO RR Club
  10, 11, 13, 16, 17, 18, 22, 30, 38
Switch, Lap 28
  Single-point 26
  Slip 28
  Split 26
  Stub 26
  Three way 28
  Tongue 26
Switch back 30
Switching lead 43
Switching line 6, 43

TOFC 53
Table benchwork 10
Table-top benchwork 9
Team track 52
Template 25, 28, 35, 44
Terminal 43
Terminal RR 5
The Model RR Club 4, 9, 13, 16, 17,
  19, 22, 27, 30, 35, 39, 47, 50, 54, 56, 64
Three-way switch 28
Through station 47
Throat 49
Track, Ash 59
  Caboose 57
  Centers 32
  Classification 55
  Coal 59
  Crossing 29
  Crossover 26
  Departure 55
  Diagram 40
  Holding 53
  House 52
  Icing 57
  Industrial 54
  Interchange 22, 52
  Lead 55
  Local order 55
  Main 35, 36